# Mastering Data Science and Big Data Analytics

**Mastering Big Data:
Strategies and Tools for Effective Analysis**

# Maxine Chen

# Table of Contents

# INTRODUCTION

In the digital age, data has become the lifeblood of industries, governments, and organizations of all sizes. The era of big data has emerged due to the exponential growth of information collected from many sources and the development of advanced technology. This revolutionary phenomenon can completely change how we think, act, and understand in a wide range of fields.

Welcome to " Mastering Data Science and Big Data Analytics: Mastering Big Data - Strategies and Tools for Effective Analysis." We explore the field of data science and its ever-changing interaction with big data in this book. We will help you understand the intricacies of this quickly developing subject and provide you with the skills, tactics, and resources you need to use big data for insightful research.

Data is becoming more than just a result of our digital interactions; it is a strategic tool that improves our daily lives, drives business decisions, and informs policymaking. Every swipe, click, sensor reading, and social media post adds to the ever-growing digital world. This wealth of information offers unprecedented opportunities yet presents formidable challenges.

The challenges of organizing, processing, and deriving valuable insights from data are growing exponentially. Traditional approaches of analysis are overwhelmed by the sheer volume, velocity, as well as variety of data. Without the appropriate tactics and resources, businesses run the risk of becoming lost in a sea of data and unable to utilize its potential fully. Big data analysis methods and data science concepts come into play here.

The purpose of this book is to serve as a guide for you as you navigate the complex world of big data analysis and data science. Gain a thorough understanding of how to efficiently leverage the potential of big data, from grasping basic ideas to mastering sophisticated methodologies. There will be extensive coverage of a variety of topics, such as preprocessing, exploratory data analysis, analytics techniques, data collection and storage, visualization, and more.

You will find a combination of case studies, theoretical insights, real-world examples, and practical advice in the following pages. Whether you're a business professional looking to use data-driven insights, an aspiring data scientist, or just curious about the revolutionary power of big data, this book seeks to provide you with the information and abilities required to succeed in this dynamic and quickly developing industry.

Let's go on this journey to become experts in big data, analyze tactics, and investigate tools for efficient data analysis. Upon finishing the book, you will possess the knowledge necessary to successfully navigate the intricate realm of data science and utilize big data to inform decisions and spur creativity.

# CHAPTER I

# Understanding Big Data

## Definition and characteristics of big data

In the digital era, the term "big data" has emerged as a buzzword, representing a seismic shift in how we collect, process, and interpret information. Big data refers to the colossal and complex datasets that exceed the processing capabilities of traditional database management systems. These datasets are generated from diverse sources, including sensors, social media platforms, online transactions, etc. At the heart of the big data phenomenon lies the challenge of managing the sheer volume of data and harnessing its velocity, variety, veracity, and value.

Volume, the first characteristic of big data, refers to the sheer magnitude of information generated daily. The volume of data is staggering, measured in petabytes and exabytes, and it continues to expand exponentially. Think about the massive volume of data generated by wearables, industrial sensors, smart appliances, and other Internet of Things (IoT) devices. This influx of data necessitates novel storage, processing, and analysis approaches that can handle such immense quantities.

Velocity underscores the speed at which data is generated, collected, and shared. Social media platforms, for instance, create an avalanche of real-time updates, interactions, and posts. Financial markets produce a torrent of transactions in milliseconds. The ability to capture, process, and act upon data in real-time is a defining feature of big data applications. Analyzing data as it is generated allows organizations to make informed decisions swiftly and respond to emerging trends promptly.

Variety encompasses the diverse types and formats of data that big data encompasses. Data comes in structured, semi-structured, and also unstructured forms. Structured data adheres to a well-defined schema, like traditional relational databases. Semi-structured data includes information that doesn't fit neatly into rows and columns, often represented in formats like JSON or XML. Unstructured data, which constitutes a significant portion of big data, includes text, images, audio, and video. The ability to extract important insights from this heterogeneous mix of data requires sophisticated analytical techniques and tools.

Veracity, while not as commonly discussed as other characteristics, is equally important. The accuracy and reliability of the data are related to veracity. Ensuring data quality becomes a challenge with the deluge of information from various sources. Data might be incomplete, inconsistent, or even intentionally misleading. Ensuring data veracity involves implementing robust data validation and quality control processes to minimize erroneous analyses and misguided decisions.

Value is the ultimate goal of big data analysis. Amidst the sea of information, organizations seek to extract valuable insights that can drive innovation, enhance decision-making, and improve operational efficiency. The value derived from big data can manifest in various ways, from optimizing supply chains and predicting customer preferences to improving healthcare outcomes and aiding scientific research.

In the pursuit of extracting value from big data, three additional characteristics have emerged that complement the 5 Vs: Variability, Complexity, and Privacy. Variability refers to the inconsistency of data flows. Data can arrive at irregular intervals, making it challenging to predict and manage. Complexity arises from the intricacies of dealing with diverse data sources, formats, and analytical methods. The more complex the data landscape, the greater the need for advanced tools and expertise. Privacy, a critical concern in the digital age, pertains to protecting sensitive and personally identifiable information. With vast amounts of data circulating, safeguarding privacy while leveraging data for analysis poses significant ethical and regulatory challenges.

In conclusion, big data has transformed how we perceive, process, and interpret information. Its characteristics of volume, velocity, variety, veracity, and value underpin its essence. As we delve deeper into the digital age, understanding and harnessing big data's potential becomes pivotal for individuals, organizations, and societies at large. The ability to extract important insights from this data deluge offers unprecedented opportunities for innovation, informed decision-making, and progress across myriad domains.

## Importance of big data in various industries

In the age of digital transformation, data has emerged as a valuable currency that fuels innovation, informs decision-making, and shapes the trajectory of industries worldwide. Big data, characterized by its immense volume, velocity, and variety, has revolutionized how businesses and organizations operate across diverse sectors. The ability to capture, process, and analyze vast amounts of data has led to a paradigm shift, unlocking new opportunities and transforming traditional practices in numerous industries.

Healthcare, once reliant on paper-based records and limited patient information, has experienced a monumental transformation through big data. Electronic health records (EHRs) and wearable devices generate unprecedented patient data. This influx of information has enabled personalized treatment plans, predictive analytics for disease outbreaks, and early detection of medical conditions through data-driven insights.

Moreover, genomics research and pharmaceutical development increasingly rely on big data analytics to identify genetic markers, model drug interactions, and accelerate the pace of medical discoveries.
In the Retail sector, big data has redefined how businesses understand and engage with customers.

Customer interactions, purchase history, and browsing patterns provide valuable insights for targeted marketing campaigns, personalized recommendations, and optimizing inventory management. Retailers utilize big data analytics to anticipate trends, adjust pricing strategies, and enhance customer experience. Integrating e-commerce platforms with data analytics has ushered in an era of data-driven retail, allowing companies to stay competitive and agile in a quickly evolving market.

The Financial Services industry has also undergone a seismic transformation through the power of big data. Traditionally, financial institutions relied on historical data for risk assessment and decision-making. However, the emergence of big data analytics enables real-time monitoring of market trends, sentiment analysis of social media data, and fraud detection using machine learning algorithms. These capabilities enhance risk management, fraud prevention, and investment strategies, ultimately leading to more informed and agile financial operations.

In the realm of Manufacturing, big data is revolutionizing production processes and supply chain management. Integrating sensors and IoT devices in manufacturing facilities generates real-time data on equipment performance, energy consumption, and quality control. This data-driven approach enables predictive maintenance, reducing downtime and optimizing production efficiency. Supply chains are further enhanced by leveraging big data to track and optimize inventory, anticipate demand fluctuations, and minimize operational disruptions.

The field of Transportation has embraced big data to enhance mobility and improve infrastructure. Smart cities utilize data from sensors and GPS devices to optimize traffic flow, reduce congestion, and improve public transportation systems. Ride-sharing platforms use big data to match drivers with passengers efficiently and predict demand patterns. Additionally, big data analysis contributes to the development of autonomous vehicles by processing and interpreting the huge quantity of data generated by sensors and cameras.

In the Energy sector, big data is crucial in achieving sustainability and efficiency goals. Smart grids equipped with sensors and meters provide real-time data on energy consumption patterns, enabling better distribution and utilization of resources. Energy companies leverage big data analytics to predict maintenance needs in power plants, optimize energy production, and identify opportunities for energy conservation.

The Agriculture industry has witnessed a transformation by applying big data analytics, leading to precision farming practices. Sensors, drones, and satellite imagery collect data on soil conditions, weather patterns, and crop health. This data is then analyzed to make informed irrigation, fertilizer application, and pest management decisions. Precision agriculture improves crop yields and resource utilization and promotes sustainable farming practices.

In the field of Entertainment and Media, big data has revolutionized content creation, distribution, and audience engagement. Streaming platforms analyze user preferences and viewing habits to recommend personalized content, enhancing user experiences and retention rates. Big data analytics also help content creators understand audience reactions, allowing for iterative improvements and targeted marketing campaigns.

The Public Sector is leveraging big data to enhance governance, service delivery, and policy-making. Government agencies utilize data analytics to address urban challenges, optimize public services, and to improve emergency response systems. Big data is crucial in analyzing census data, tracking disease outbreaks, and monitoring environmental indicators to inform evidence-based policies that benefit society as a whole.

In conclusion, big data has become a driving force that transcends industry boundaries, reshaping the landscape of businesses and organizations. Its impact spans healthcare, retail, finance, manufacturing, transportation, energy, agriculture, entertainment, and the public sector. By harnessing the power of big data, industries can make informed decisions, unlock new efficiencies, drive innovation, and provide enhanced experiences for customers and stakeholders. With the world being more data-driven and interconnected, embracing big data analytics has become advantageous and essential for industries to thrive and adapt in the evolving digital age.

## Types of data: structured, semi-structured, and unstructured

In the vast landscape of the digital age, data is the cornerstone of information and insights. However, not all data is created equal. The classification of data into structured, semi-structured, and unstructured categories provides a framework for understanding the diverse forms and complexities of the information that permeates our digital world. Each data type carries distinct characteristics, challenges, and opportunities, shaping how organizations collect, store, process, and derive value from their data assets.

Structured Data, the most traditional and organized form of data, adheres to a well-defined schema. It is typically stored in relational databases where each piece of data is assigned to a specific field or column. Structured data is highly organized, making it suitable for systematic queries, analysis, and reporting. Examples of structured data include transaction records, customer profiles, financial statements, and inventory lists. The tabular format of structured data enables easy integration and consistency, simplifying data management and enabling efficient data manipulation.

Semi-structured data presents a middle ground between the rigid structure of structured data and the free-form nature of unstructured data. In this type, data elements are organized into a format that captures their relationships and hierarchies. Unlike structured data, semi-structured data allows for variations in the data model. One common representation of semi-structured data is the Extensible Markup Language (XML), where tags define data elements and their relationships. JSON (JavaScript Object Notation) is another widely used format for semi-structured data, frequently employed in web applications and APIs. Semi-structured data accommodates evolving data structures and can capture complex information, making it adaptable to scenarios where data schemas may evolve over time.

Unstructured Data starkly contrasts the organized formats of structured and semi-structured data. This data type lacks a predefined structure or schema, presenting itself in raw and diverse forms. Unstructured data encompasses a wide array of information, including text documents, images, audio files, video clips, social media posts, and sensor data. Its lack of inherent organization poses challenges for traditional data management and analysis methods. However, the potential insights within unstructured data are immense, making it a treasure trove for data scientists and organizations seeking to extract value from the information deluge.

Structured, semi-structured, and unstructured data each have distinct attributes influencing their applications and challenges. Structured data's organized nature enables easy storage, retrieval, and analysis, making it ideal for tasks that require systematic querying and reporting. For instance, financial institutions rely on structured data to manage transactions and generate accurate reports. On the other hand, semi-structured data bridges the gap between structured and unstructured data, catering to scenarios where data models are flexible and evolving.

Organizations employing web services often utilize semi-structured data formats like XML or JSON to exchange information between systems.

Unstructured data's complexity and diversity offer untapped potential for insights that may not be discernible through traditional analysis methods. Natural language processing (NLP) techniques can extract meaning from text documents, sentiment analysis can gauge public sentiment from social media posts, and image recognition algorithms can derive insights from images and videos. For instance, analyzing unstructured patient records using NLP can lead to early disease detection and personalized treatment recommendations in the healthcare industry.

Organizations are embracing advanced technologies and techniques to harness the potential of these diverse data types effectively. Data warehouses and relational databases are tailored for structured data, while NoSQL databases and data lakes are employed for storing and analyzing semi-structured and unstructured data. Advanced analytics tools, machine learning algorithms, as well as artificial intelligence models enable the extraction of insights from all data types, regardless of their format.

In conclusion, classifying data into structured, semi-structured, and unstructured categories provides a lens through which we can understand the rich tapestry of information in the digital age. Structured data offers organization and efficiency, semi-structured data bridges flexibility and structure, and unstructured data presents challenges and opportunities for innovation. As organizations strive to make informed decisions and uncover hidden insights, the interplay between these data types will continue to shape the landscape of data management, analysis, and application across industries.

## 3Vs of big data: Volume, Velocity, Variety

In the digital age, data has evolved from a mere byproduct of technological interactions to a strategic asset that drives innovation, informs decision-making, and transforms industries. As the volume and diversity of data generated continue to soar, traditional data management and analysis approaches are rendered inadequate. The concept of the 3 Vs of big data—Volume, Velocity, and Variety—emerges as a fundamental framework to capture the distinct challenges posed by the deluge of information in today's interconnected world. These three characteristics highlight the essence of big data, providing insights into its complexity and offering a roadmap for organizations seeking to extract meaningful value from their data assets.

Volume, the first of the 3 Vs, underscores the sheer magnitude of data that organizations and individuals generate, collect, and share daily. The explosion of data volume is a hallmark of the digital revolution, with estimates of data growth reaching staggering proportions—measured in zettabytes and beyond. This influx of data emanates from diverse sources, including sensors, social media platforms, mobile devices, and Internet of Things (IoT) devices. The ability to store and process such immense quantities of data poses unprecedented challenges to traditional storage and computational methods.

This voluminous data brings forth both opportunities and dilemmas. The opportunities lie in the potential insights that can be gleaned from this data wealth. Organizations can analyze consumer behavior patterns, predict market trends, optimize supply chains, and personalize user experiences. However, the sheer volume of data can overwhelm existing infrastructure, necessitating scalable solutions such as distributed computing and cloud storage. Efficient data management systems and technologies like Hadoop and Spark have emerged to address the challenges of volume, allowing organizations to store, process, and analyze large datasets effectively.

Velocity, the second V, characterizes the speed at which data is generated, collected, and disseminated. Data flows continuously and rapidly in a world of real-time interactions and instant connectivity. Social media platforms generate constant updates, financial markets execute trades within milliseconds, and sensors in manufacturing facilities produce data at high frequencies. Organizations must be equipped to capture and process this torrent of data in real time to remain competitive and agile in their decision-making.

The velocity of data has profound implications for diverse industries. In financial services, real-time data feeds enable high-frequency trading and risk assessment. In healthcare, wearable devices and remote patient monitoring generate constant streams of health-related data. The transportation sector leverages real-time data from GPS devices and traffic sensors to optimize route planning and enhance urban mobility. Addressing the challenges of velocity requires robust data streaming technologies and real-time analytics platforms that can handle the rapid flow of information and provide insights in the moment.

Variety, the third V, speaks to the heterogeneous nature of data. Data comes in myriad forms, ranging from structured data with predefined formats to unstructured data in the form of text, images, audio, as well as video. Semi-structured data, which falls between these two extremes, includes data with partial structure and varying levels of organization. This diversity of data formats poses challenges in storage, processing, and analysis.

The variety of data sources and formats calls for adaptive data management and analysis approaches. Traditional relational databases are well-suited for structured data, but they may struggle to handle the complexity of semi-structured and unstructured data. NoSQL databases, data lakes, and data warehouses have emerged as solutions tailored to different data types. Organizations leverage natural language processing, image recognition, and text analysis technologies to derive insights from unstructured data sources. Variety-driven challenges also extend to data integration, as organizations strive to combine data from disparate sources to create a comprehensive view of their operations and customers.

While the 3 Vs of big data—Volume, Velocity, and Variety—provide a foundational framework for understanding the challenges posed by the data revolution, it is worth noting that these Vs have evolved over time. Some framework variations introduce additional Vs, such as Veracity (ensuring data quality and accuracy) and Value (extracting meaningful insights). These extensions acknowledge the increasing complexity of the big data landscape and the need for robust solutions to address emerging challenges.

In conclusion, the 3 Vs of big data serve as pillars of insight into the dynamic and multifaceted nature of data in the modern era. Volume, Velocity, and Variety collectively define the challenges and opportunities of the data deluge. Organizations that embrace these characteristics and deploy innovative technologies and strategies are better positioned to navigate the complexities of big data and harness its potential to drive innovation, make informed decisions, and fuel growth in an interconnected and data-driven world.

## Real-world examples of big data applications

In the digital age, data has transcended its role as a passive byproduct of interactions and transactions, evolving into a transformative force that shapes industries, informs decisions, and revolutionizes processes. The application of big data analytics has emerged as a game-changer across diverse sectors, illuminating the immense potential within the voluminous and dynamic information streams that define our modern world. Real-world examples of big data applications demonstrate how organizations leverage data to gain insights, make informed decisions, and drive innovation across domains as varied as healthcare, retail, finance, and beyond.

Healthcare, a sector defined by complex patient information, treatment plans, and research endeavors, has experienced a paradigm shift through big data applications. Electronic Health Records (EHRs) and wearable devices generate many patient data, providing a holistic view of health conditions and treatment outcomes. By analyzing this data, healthcare providers can determine trends, personalize treatment plans, and even predict disease outbreaks. For instance, Google's Flu Trends project harnessed search data to predict flu outbreaks more accurately than traditional surveillance methods. Moreover, the application of big data in genomics research has accelerated discoveries related to genetic markers, leading to advancements in precision medicine and tailored therapies.

Big data analytics has fundamentally transformed retail, enhancing customer experiences, optimizing supply chains, and driving business growth. E-commerce platforms analyze customer interactions, purchase history, and browsing patterns to recommend personalized products and improve user engagement. Retailers employ big data to optimize inventory management by predicting demand fluctuations and reducing stockouts. Amazon, a pioneer in using data analytics, utilizes predictive analytics to anticipate customer preferences, resulting in more effective cross-selling and upselling strategies. The power of big data in retail lies in its ability to make a seamless and personalized shopping experience for consumers.

Big data applications have redefined risk management, fraud detection, and investment strategies in the Financial Services sector. Traditional approaches to risk assessment are supplemented by real-time data streams that capture market trends and sentiment analysis from social media. For example, hedge funds and investment firms leverage big data analytics to make informed decisions based on real-time market insights. Moreover, credit scoring models are becoming more accurate by incorporating alternative data sources, such as social media behavior and transaction history, to assess an individual's creditworthiness beyond conventional credit scores.

Manufacturing has undergone a technological revolution by integrating big data analytics into production processes and supply chain management. The deployment of sensors and IoT devices in manufacturing facilities generates real-time data on equipment performance, energy consumption, and quality control. This data is analyzed to enable predictive maintenance, minimizing downtime and optimizing production efficiency. General Electric's "Brilliant Factory" initiative is a testament to the transformative power of big data in manufacturing, using data analytics to streamline operations, reduce costs, and enhance overall productivity.

In Transportation, big data is driving innovation in urban mobility, logistics, and vehicle safety. Smart cities analyze real-time data from sensors and GPS devices to optimize traffic flow, reduce congestion, and improve public transportation services. Ride-sharing platforms use big data algorithms to match drivers with passengers efficiently, contributing to reduced traffic and enhanced convenience. The rise of autonomous vehicles is also fueled by big data analytics, as these vehicles process massive amounts of sensor data to navigate safely and efficiently.

The Energy industry has harnessed big data applications to achieve sustainability and operational efficiency goals. Smart grids with sensors and meters provide real-time data on energy consumption patterns, facilitating effective distribution and resource utilization. Big data analytics enable energy companies to predict maintenance needs in power plants, optimize energy production, and identify opportunities for energy conservation. The Pacific Gas and Electric Company, for example, utilizes big data to identify inefficiencies in energy distribution and enhance customer service.

In the realm of Agriculture, big data applications have given rise to precision farming practices. Sensors, drones, and satellite imagery collect data on soil conditions, weather patterns, and crop health. This data is analyzed to optimize irrigation, fertilizer application, and pest management, leading to increased yields and resource efficiency. John Deere's "FarmSight" initiative employs big data analytics to provide farmers with real-time insights to enhance decision-making and maximize agricultural productivity.

In the Entertainment and Media context, big data shapes content creation, distribution, and audience engagement. Streaming platforms analyze user preferences and viewing habits to recommend personalized content, driving user retention and satisfaction. Media companies utilize big data analytics to tailor advertising campaigns and content strategies to specific target audiences, increasing effectiveness and revenue.

The Public Sector harnesses big data applications to enhance governance, service delivery, and policy-making. Government agencies analyze data to address urban challenges, optimize public services, and improve emergency response systems. For instance, the City of Chicago uses big data to predict potential rat infestations based on complaints and environmental conditions, allowing for proactive pest control measures. Additionally, big data analytics are instrumental in monitoring disease outbreaks, tracking census data, and managing transportation infrastructure.

In conclusion, real-world examples of big data applications underscore the transformative potential of data analytics across diverse industries. Big data is reshaping how organizations operate, make decisions, and innovate from healthcare and retail to finance, manufacturing, transportation, energy, agriculture, entertainment, and the public sector. The application of big data analytics enables personalized experiences, optimized processes, enhanced decision-making, and innovative breakthroughs that contribute to the advancement of society as a whole. As the data landscape continues to evolve, the lessons and successes of these real-world examples serve as a testament to the boundless opportunities that await those who embrace the power of big data.

# CHAPTER II

# Fundamentals of Data Science

## Introduction to data science and its role in analyzing big data

In an era marked by an unprecedented surge in data generation and consumption, data science has emerged as a linchpin in understanding, extracting insights, and deriving value from the vast and intricate web of information that permeates our digital landscape. Data science, often hailed as the art and science of uncovering meaningful patterns from data, has become a catalyst for innovation, informing strategic decisions and propelling organizations toward success. This section delves into the essence of data science, its foundational components, and its pivotal role in analyzing big data—a task that is characterized by immense volume, velocity, and variety.

Data science is a multidisciplinary field encompassing a wide spectrum of skills, techniques, and methodologies to transform raw data into actionable insights. It stands at the intersection of statistics, computer science, domain expertise, and communication, weaving together quantitative analysis with qualitative understanding to unearth hidden truths and trends within data. At its core, data science bridges the gap between the vast amounts of information available and the human capacity to interpret and utilize it effectively.

Data science involves a holistic approach encompassing various stages of the data lifecycle. The foundation of data science rests on Data Collection, where diverse sources of information are harnessed to build comprehensive datasets. This step involves data acquisition, cleaning, and ensuring data quality and integrity—a process laying the groundwork for accurate analysis.

Following data collection, Data Preprocessing plays a pivotal role in preparing data for analysis. This involves handling missing values, outlier detection, and data transformation to ensure that the data is in a suitable format for analysis. Data preprocessing is vital as it directly impacts the accuracy and reliability of subsequent analyses.

Exploratory Data Analysis (EDA) is another vital component of data science, involving the examination of data distributions, correlations, and patterns. Visualization techniques are often employed to convey insights in an accessible and meaningful manner. EDA helps data scientists gain a deeper understanding of the data and identify potential avenues for further analysis.

At the heart of data science lies Model Building and Machine Learning, where statistical and machine learning techniques are applied to data to create predictive models and uncover insights. Machine learning algorithms, ranging from linear regression to complex neural networks, enable data scientists to discover patterns, make predictions, and automate decision-making processes.

Finally, the insights and findings obtained from the analysis are communicated through Data Visualization and Communication. Effective visualization techniques transform complex data into visually engaging representations that both technical and non-technical stakeholders can readily understand. The ability to convey insights through compelling visualizations is crucial for informing decision-makers and driving actionable outcomes.

The advent of big data has amplified the role of data science, underscoring its significance in extracting value from the massive and heterogeneous datasets that characterize the digital landscape. Big data, often defined by the 3 Vs—Volume, Velocity, and Variety—presents challenges that transcend the capabilities of traditional data processing methods.

Volume signifies the sheer magnitude of data generated from diverse sources such as sensors, social media platforms, and IoT devices. Handling and analyzing such vast quantities of data demands scalable techniques to process and extract insights from this data deluge efficiently. Data science equips professionals with the tools to manage and analyze massive datasets, identifying meaningful patterns even within the noise of voluminous information.

Velocity emphasizes the rapid rate at which data is generated and shared in real time. Social media interactions, financial transactions, and sensor readings occur astonishingly, necessitating real-time analysis to derive immediate insights. Data science techniques, including streaming analytics and real-time processing, enable organizations to make informed decisions in the moment, whether it's optimizing supply chains, tracking customer sentiment, or detecting anomalies.

Variety underscores the diverse forms and formats of data, spanning structured, semi-structured, and unstructured data types. Unstructured data, like text, images, and videos, constitutes a significant portion of big data and requires specialized techniques to extract insights. Data science equips professionals with the skills to process and analyze various data types, ensuring the full spectrum of information is leveraged for analysis.

In conclusion, data science stands as the linchpin in analyzing and interpreting big data—a transformative force that propels organizations toward innovation and informed decision-making. By combining statistical rigor, domain expertise, and technological prowess, data science professionals wield the power to unlock insights from the vast expanse of data available. As the digital landscape evolves, the role of data science will remain pivotal in deciphering the intricacies of big data and steering organizations toward success in an increasingly data-driven world.


## Data science lifecycle: CRISP-DM framework

In the realm of data science, where the pursuit of insights and knowledge intersects with the intricacies of data, a systematic and structured approach is essential to navigate the complex journey from raw data to actionable insights. The CRISP-DM framework (Cross-Industry Standard Process for Data Mining) has emerged as a guiding beacon in the data science landscape, providing a comprehensive roadmap that outlines the key stages and tasks involved in the data science lifecycle. This section delves into the intricacies of the CRISP-DM framework, shedding light on its six distinct phases and highlighting its significance in transforming data into valuable insights.

CRISP-DM is a cyclical and iterative process encompassing six interrelated phases: Business

Understanding, Data Understanding, Data Preparation, Modeling, Evaluation, and Deployment. Each phase is characterized by specific tasks and activities, ensuring the data science process remains systematic, comprehensive, and focused on addressing business objectives.

Business Understanding: At the heart of the CRISP-DM framework lies the recognition that business goals and challenges fundamentally drive data science. In this phase, data scientists collaborate closely with domain experts and stakeholders to gain a deep understanding of the business context, objectives, and requirements. Identifying the problem to be solved and the opportunities to be pursued sets the stage for all subsequent stages of the data science lifecycle.

Data Understanding: With a clear business understanding, the next step involves comprehending the available data resources. Data scientists explore and analyze the data to uncover its structure, quality, and relevance to the problem at hand. Data profiling, summary statistics, and data visualization techniques aid in gaining insights into the data's characteristics and potential challenges.

Data Preparation: Often hailed as one of the most time-consuming phases, data preparation involves cleaning, transforming, and structuring the data to facilitate analysis. Data cleaning entails dealing with missing values, outliers, and inconsistencies that can skew results. Data transformation involves converting data into suitable formats and aggregating it as needed. Ensuring data quality and consistency is paramount in this phase, as the accuracy of subsequent analyses hinges on the integrity of the data.

Modeling: Data scientists leverage statistical and machine learning methods to create models during the modeling phase that address the business problem. This phase is where predictive and analytical models are created using algorithms such as regression, clustering, and neural networks. Data scientists refine and tune the models to ensure they accurately capture patterns and relationships within the data. Experimentation and iteration are key as various approaches are explored to achieve optimal model performance.

Evaluation: With models in place, the evaluation phase assesses their effectiveness and performance. Data scientists use validation and testing methods to measure how well the models generalize to new, unseen data. Evaluation metrics like accuracy, precision, and recall provide quantitative measures of model performance. The goal is to select the best-performing model that aligns with the business objectives and minimizes the risk of overfitting.

Deployment: After a thorough evaluation, the selected model is deployed into the operational environment. Deployment involves integrating the model into existing systems, making it accessible to end-users or stakeholders. Monitoring the deployed model's performance is essential to ensure it continues to deliver accurate results over time. Iterative improvement and updates may be required to adapt to changing data and business requirements.

The CRISP-DM framework's significance lies in its ability to provide structure and clarity to the inherently iterative and multifaceted data science process. Its cyclical nature emphasizes that data science is not a linear path but an ongoing journey requiring continuous refinement and adaptation. The framework's systematic approach ensures that no crucial step is overlooked, from understanding business goals to deploying actionable insights.

CRISP-DM's adaptability makes it well-suited for various industries and domains. Its flexibility allows data scientists to tailor the framework to specific projects while maintaining a consistent methodology. Whether solving complex business problems, optimizing processes, or driving innovation, the CRISP-DM framework is a reliable roadmap that guides data scientists through the intricacies of the data science lifecycle.

Real-world applications of the CRISP-DM framework span industries and domains, demonstrating its versatility and effectiveness. For instance, in the Retail sector, CRISP-DM aids in understanding customer behavior patterns, optimizing inventory management, and developing targeted marketing strategies. In the Healthcare domain, the framework assists in predicting disease outbreaks, personalizing treatment plans, and improving patient outcomes. CRISP-DM is utilized for fraud detection, risk assessment, and investment strategies in the Financial Services industry.

Moreover, the CRISP-DM framework's iterative nature aligns with the scientific method's principles, emphasizing hypothesis testing, experimentation, and refinement. Data scientists iterate through the phases, adjusting models, evaluating results, and deploying insights, mirroring the iterative nature of scientific inquiry.

In conclusion, the CRISP-DM framework has emerged as a cornerstone in the data science landscape, providing a structured and systematic approach to transforming data into actionable insights. Its six phases—Business Understanding, Data Understanding, Data Preparation,

Modeling, Evaluation, and Deployment—guide data scientists through the complexities of the data science lifecycle. With its cyclical nature and adaptability, CRISP-DM empowers organizations across industries to uncover patterns, drive innovation, and make informed decisions based on the information available. As the digital age continues to evolve, the CRISP-DM framework remains a steadfast companion in deriving value from data and transforming it into meaningful insights that propel organizations toward success.

## Role of data scientists and their skill set

Within the rapidly evolving digital age environment, where data serves as the currency of innovation and insight, the role of data scientists has emerged as indispensable to organizations seeking to harness the potential of their information assets. Data scientists are the architects of knowledge, transforming raw data into actionable insights that drive strategic decisions, foster innovation, and unlock competitive advantages.

At the core of their role, data scientists bridge the gap between data and understanding, leveraging advanced analytical techniques and domain expertise to extract valuable insights from complex datasets. Their responsibilities span a spectrum of activities encompassing problem-solving, data wrangling, model development, and communication of findings.

The journey of a data scientist begins with Problem Definition, understanding and defining the business problem or question at hand. By collaborating closely with domain experts and stakeholders, data scientists ensure that their analyses align with the strategic objectives and needs of the organization.

Data Collection and Preparation involves the critical responsibility of collecting, cleaning, as well as preparing data for analysis. This meticulous process includes identifying relevant data sources, handling missing values, and transforming data into formats suitable for analysis.

Exploratory Data Analysis (EDA) is a crucial phase where data scientists use visualization and statistical techniques to gain insights into data distributions, relationships, and potential patterns. EDA lays the foundation for subsequent modeling and analysis, helping data scientists uncover vital insights and hypotheses that guide their work.

Data scientists utilize statistical and machine learning techniques to build predictive and analytical models in the Model Development and Machine Learning phase. The process involves selecting appropriate algorithms, training models on data, tuning parameters, and evaluating model performance.

Evaluation and Interpretation involve rigorously evaluating model performance to ensure they generalize well to new data. Interpretation of model results is a crucial skill, as data scientists must communicate complex findings clearly and promptly to stakeholders.

The insights derived from data analysis are valuable only when they are translated into actionable outcomes. Data scientists play a pivotal role in Deployment and Communication, integrating models into business processes and facilitating their use by decision-makers. Effective communication skills are vital in presenting findings to technical and non-technical audiences.

The role of data scientists demands a diverse skill set that combines technical expertise, domain knowledge, and effective communication. Programming Languages like Python and R are essential for data manipulation and analysis. A strong foundation in Statistical Analysis guides data scientists in making informed decisions and drawing meaningful insights from data.

Understanding machine learning concepts and algorithms empowers data scientists to develop predictive and analytical models. Data Visualization skills allow data scientists to present complex findings in a visual and accessible format.

Domain Expertise enables data scientists to ask relevant questions, tailor analyses to specific needs, and interpret findings in context. Proficiency in Data Management ensures data quality and availability for analysis.
Clear Problem-Solving abilities, combined with effective Communication skills, form the backbone of a successful data scientist's toolkit.

The role of data scientists extends beyond individual projects; it profoundly impacts shaping the data-driven future of organizations and industries. By harnessing data to make informed decisions, drive innovation, and optimize processes, data scientists contribute to organizations' growth and resilience in a rapidly changing landscape.

In conclusion, data scientists' role is dynamic and pivotal in the modern era. With their ability to transform data into insights, data scientists empower organizations to make informed decisions, drive innovation, and adapt to evolving challenges. As organizations navigate the complexities of the digital age, data scientists will remain at the forefront of turning data into actionable insights that shape industries, drive progress, and unlock new possibilities.

## Ethical considerations in data science

In the era of unprecedented data availability and advanced analytics, the power of data science to drive innovation, inform decision-making, and transform industries is undeniable. However, with great power comes great responsibility, and the ethical considerations surrounding data science have come to the forefront of discussions about data's responsible and equitable use. As data scientists wield the ability to extract insights from vast datasets that often contain personal and sensitive information, it is imperative to navigate the ethical dimensions of data science to ensure that technology benefits society while avoiding harm. This section explores the multifaceted ethical considerations in data science, ranging from privacy and bias to transparency and accountability.

One of the foremost ethical concerns in data science revolves around privacy and the collection of personal data. As organizations gather data from diverse sources, including social media, sensors, and online transactions, individuals' privacy is at risk of being compromised. The challenge lies in balancing the utility of data for analysis and the need to obtain informed consent from individuals whose data is being used. Ethical data collection entails transparency about the purposes of data usage, the ability to opt-out, and ensuring that data is anonymized and protected from unauthorized access. Stricter regulations, like the GDPR (General Data Protection Regulation), highlight the growing emphasis on safeguarding individuals' privacy and giving them control over their data.

Data science holds the promise of objective insights, yet it is susceptible to bias that can perpetuate societal inequalities. Biased data inputs, such as historical biases in training data, can lead to biased model outputs, thereby reinforcing discrimination and inequities. Ensuring fairness requires diligent examination of training data and model outcomes to identify and mitigate biases. Transparent reporting of model performance across diverse groups is essential to prevent the exacerbation of existing inequalities. By adopting techniques that promote fairness, such as adversarial training and re-sampling, data scientists can mitigate bias and contribute to more equitable outcomes.

As data science models become increasingly complex, transparency and explainability emerge as ethical imperatives. Stakeholders, including end-users, regulators, and the public, must understand how models arrive at decisions. Black-box models, which produce results without clear explanations, raise concerns about accountability and potential biases. Addressing this ethical consideration involves employing interpretable models, generating explanations for predictions, and adopting practices like "algorithmic transparency." By fostering trust through transparent practices, data scientists can ensure that their models are accountable and understandable to all stakeholders.

Ethical considerations in data science extend to the broader responsibilities of data scientists, organizations, and regulatory bodies. Data breaches, unintended consequences of algorithms, and misinterpretation of results underscore the need for accountability. Data scientists should adhere to ethical guidelines, codes of conduct, and best practices that promote responsible behavior. Organizations must implement robust governance frameworks that ensure ethical data collection, handling, and analysis. Regulatory bodies are crucial in setting standards and enforcing ethical practices, ensuring that data science operates within ethical boundaries.

As data science continues to evolve, emerging technologies like artificial intelligence (AI), machine learning, and deep learning introduce novel ethical challenges. The potential for AI to make autonomous decisions raises questions about accountability when machines make choices that impact individuals' lives.

Ethical considerations encompass ensuring that AI systems are transparent, fair, and aligned with human values. Ethical discussions also extend to futuristic scenarios such as AI-generated content, deepfakes, and autonomous vehicles, necessitating a proactive approach to recognizing and addressing ethical concerns.

The responsibility of ethical data science lies not only in regulation and oversight but also in the ethical literacy of data scientists themselves. It is crucial to educate data scientists about the potential ethical pitfalls, biases, and implications of their work. Ethics should be integrated into data science curricula, emphasizing the importance of considering societal impacts, respecting privacy, and addressing bias. By fostering ethical awareness and accountability, education empowers data scientists to approach their work responsibly toward the data and the people it represents.

In conclusion, ethical considerations in data science are intrinsic to the responsible use of technology in the modern world. Data scientists play a pivotal role in navigating these considerations, as they influence the collection, analysis, and interpretation of data that shapes decisions across industries. By prioritizing privacy, addressing bias, ensuring transparency, and embracing accountability, data scientists contribute to a data-driven future that respects individuals' rights, promotes fairness, and builds trust. As technology advances, the ethical considerations in data science remain a vital compass guiding the responsible and equitable evolution of data-driven innovation.

# CHAPTER III

# Data Collection and Storage

## Data collection methods: sensors, social media, IoT devices, etc.

In the digital age, where data serves as the fuel that powers innovation, understanding data collection methods is fundamental to harnessing the insights that drive progress. Data collection is the cornerstone of data-driven decision-making, enabling organizations to uncover patterns, trends, and correlations that inform strategies and shape the future. This section delves into various data collection methods, ranging from sensors and social media to Internet of Things (IoT) devices, highlighting their significance, challenges, and transformative potential.

Sensors represent a ubiquitous data collection method that captures real-world phenomena through various devices. These devices, ranging from temperature sensors to accelerometers and GPS units, collect data in real-time and offer a wealth of information about physical environments and processes. For instance, weather sensors measure temperature, humidity, and atmospheric pressure, contributing to accurate weather forecasts. Industrial sensors monitor equipment performance, enabling predictive maintenance and optimization of manufacturing processes. However, sensor-based data collection presents challenges in calibration, data accuracy, and managing large volumes of real-time data streams.

Social media platforms are everywhere, and this has changed people's ability to communicate, share information, and voice opinions. Social media data collection involves gathering and analyzing user-generated content, from text posts and images to videos and interactions. This data provides valuable insights into consumer sentiment, trends, and public opinions. Social media data collection enables sentiment analysis, market research, and targeted advertising strategies. Nonetheless, ethical concerns, privacy considerations, and the potential for biases in social media data underscore the importance of responsible data collection and analysis.

An era where common things have sensors, connection, and the capacity to create and send data has been ushered in by the Internet of Things (IoT). IoT devices range from smart thermostats and wearable fitness trackers to industrial sensors and smart cities' infrastructure. IoT data collection extends beyond individuals to encompass industries, cities, and ecosystems. For example, smart cities use IoT sensors to monitor traffic flow, manage waste disposal, and optimize energy consumption. However, the proliferation of IoT devices raises concerns about data security, privacy, and interoperability, necessitating robust cybersecurity measures.

Mobile apps and wearable devices have become integral to modern lifestyles, providing individuals with tools to track health, fitness, and daily activities. These devices collect data such as heart rate, steps taken, sleep patterns, and location information. This personal data enables individuals to monitor their well-being and make informed lifestyle choices. Health-related apps and wearables, for instance, allow users to track their exercise routines and manage chronic conditions. Data accuracy, user consent, and potential health privacy breaches are among the ethical and technical challenges of mobile app and wearable data collection.

Web scraping and crawling are data collection methods that extract information from websites and online platforms. These methods allow data scientists to gather large volumes of structured as well as unstructured data for analysis. For example, e-commerce companies use web scraping to monitor competitors' prices, while researchers analyze social media data for sentiment analysis. However, legal and ethical considerations surround web scraping, as improper use can infringe on copyright, violate terms of service, and potentially disrupt websites.

Remote sensing involves using satellites, drones, and aircraft to capture data about the Earth's surface and atmosphere. Satellite imagery and remote sensing data provide insights into weather patterns, natural disasters, urban growth, and environmental changes. Remote sensing has applications in agriculture, urban planning, disaster management, and climate research. Challenges in remote sensing include data resolution, image interpretation, and ensuring data accuracy across various spectral bands.

While various data collection methods offer immense potential, they also bring forth challenges that must be addressed to ensure responsible and effective data utilization. Ensuring data accuracy, addressing biases, safeguarding privacy, and navigating legal and ethical considerations are paramount in the data collection process. Moreover, the proliferation of data sources presents the challenge of integrating disparate datasets into cohesive analyses. Additionally, as data collection technologies continue to advance, the importance of addressing digital divides and ensuring equitable access to data-driven opportunities cannot be understated.

In conclusion, data collection methods encompass diverse techniques that gather insights from the physical and digital worlds. Sensors, social media, IoT devices, mobile apps, web scraping, remote sensing, and more contribute to the data ecosystem that underpins modern decision-making and innovation. Each method offers unique advantages and challenges, shaping how organizations and individuals harness data for informed choices and transformative outcomes. As technology continues to evolve, responsible data collection practices will remain pivotal in leveraging the power of data to navigate challenges, fuel progress, and drive positive change across industries and societies.

## Data storage options: databases, data lakes, and data warehouses

In the digital age, the exponential growth of data has fueled the need for robust and efficient data storage solutions. Data lies at the heart of decision-making, innovation, and insights across industries, making the choice of storage infrastructure a critical consideration. Three prominent data storage options have emerged as cornerstones of modern data management: databases, data lakes, and data warehouses. This section delves into these storage options, exploring their characteristics, use cases, advantages, and challenges, to shed light on their role in shaping the data-driven landscape.

Databases are structured data storage solutions designed for efficient data retrieval, storage, and management. They employ a defined schema that organizes data into tables with predefined columns and data types. Structured query language, or SQL, is used by relational databases such as MySQL and PostgreSQL to manipulate and retrieve data. Databases excel at handling structured and transactional data, making them suitable for applications that require ACID (Atomicity, Consistency, Isolation, Durability) compliance, such as inventory management, e-commerce transactions, and customer relationship management (CRM) systems. The rigid structure of databases ensures data integrity and consistency, but it can limit their ability to handle diverse and unstructured data.

Data lakes are repositories that store vast amounts of raw and unstructured data in their native format. Unlike databases, data lakes accommodate various data types, including text, images, videos, logs, and sensor data, without defining a schema upfront. This flexibility makes data lakes particularly suited for big data analytics and data exploration. Data lakes, often built on distributed file systems like Hadoop HDFS, enable organizations to store and process enormous volumes of data, preparing it for downstream analysis. However, the lack of schema can lead to data quality, governance, and integration challenges, making careful data management and curation essential for effective data lake utilization.

Data warehouses are centralized repositories that aggregate data from multiple sources for analysis and reporting. They focus on structured data, consolidating information from databases, applications, and external sources into a unified schema optimized for analytics. Data warehouses like Amazon Redshift and Google

BigQuery are designed to support complex queries and enable business intelligence, data visualization, and decision support systems. They offer features like columnar storage and data compression for efficient query performance. However, data warehouses are more suitable for structured data, and their performance can degrade with concurrent complex queries or extensive data transformations.

Databases, data lakes, and data warehouses serve distinct purposes and excel in different use cases based on their characteristics. Databases are ideal for operational applications requiring structured and real-time data, like online transaction processing (OLTP) systems. Data lakes shine in scenarios where data variety, volume, and velocity are high, such as data exploration, machine learning, and big data analytics. Data warehouses are tailor-made for business intelligence, reporting, and data analytics that require querying structured data for insights.

Databases offer data integrity, ACID compliance, and fast query performance, making them suitable for transactional applications. Data lakes' flexibility accommodates diverse data types and scales, enabling organizations to store and process vast amounts of raw data. Data warehouses provide optimized query performance for structured data analysis, empowering businesses to derive insights from consolidated datasets. However, databases and data warehouses can face challenges in scaling to handle big data, and the rigidity of their structures may limit their agility. Data lakes' lack of schema can lead to data quality and governance issues, requiring careful management.

As the data storage landscape evolves, a hybrid approach that leverages the strengths of databases, data lakes, and data warehouses is gaining prominence. Organizations are adopting strategies to integrate these storage options, allowing them to combine structured and unstructured data for comprehensive analysis. This approach, known as a data lakehouse, offers the advantages of both data lakes and data warehouses, enabling agile analytics on diverse data types while maintaining the performance and querying capabilities of structured data warehouses.

In the age of data-driven decision-making, selecting the appropriate data storage solution is paramount to manage and harness the power of data effectively. Databases, data lakes, and data warehouses each bring unique characteristics and strengths to the table, catering to diverse use cases and requirements. Organizations must carefully consider their data types, velocity, and analysis needs when choosing the most suitable storage option or adopting hybrid strategies. As technology evolves, these storage options will play an integral role in shaping how organizations capture, store, and derive insights from data, paving the way for innovation and progress across industries.

## Best practices for data storage and organization

Effective data storage and organization have become essential components of modern data management strategies in the era of big data and information overload. The ability to efficiently store, manage, and retrieve data is crucial for organizations seeking to leverage data- driven insights for informed decision-making, innovation, and competitive advantage. This section delves into best data storage and organization practices, highlighting the significance of proper data management and the strategies that ensure data remains accessible, secure, and valuable.

The first step toward effective data management is selecting the appropriate data storage infrastructure. Organizations must evaluate their data requirements, including volume, velocity, variety, and access patterns, to determine the most suitable storage solution. Different data types, like structured, unstructured, and semi-structured data, may warrant distinct storage approaches. Utilizing a combination of storage options, such as databases, data lakes, and data warehouses, allows organizations to address diverse data needs while optimizing performance and cost-efficiency.

Effective data organization begins with data classification and categorization. Data should be categorized based on sensitivity, usage, and relevance. A clear taxonomy helps create a structured data storage and retrieval framework. Data classification also facilitates data lifecycle management, enabling organizations to allocate resources appropriately and apply data retention policies based on the data's value and regulatory requirements.

Metadata, or data about data, is pivotal in data organization and discoverability. Metadata includes information such as data source, creation date, owner, and description. Implementing robust metadata management practices enhances data cataloging and searchability, allowing users to locate and understand the data they need quickly. A well-maintained metadata repository streamlines collaboration, prevents data duplication, and ensures data lineage and governance.

Data governance establishes the policies, processes, and standards for data management across the organization. It encompasses data quality, security, privacy, and compliance with regulations. Implementing data governance practices ensures that data is accurate, reliable, and aligned with business objectives. Organizations should define roles and responsibilities, establish data stewardship, and enforce data access controls to maintain data integrity and meet regulatory requirements.

Data security is paramount to data storage and organization. Implementing access controls, encryption, and authentication mechanisms safeguards sensitive data from unauthorized access and breaches. The least privilege principle should be implemented by organizations, allowing access to data only to those who need it to perform their roles. Frequent vulnerability assessments and security audits assist in identifying and reducing potential risks to data assets.

Backing up data regularly and implementing robust disaster recovery plans are essential safeguards against data loss. Organizations should establish backup schedules, conduct data recovery drills, and store backups in secure and off-site locations. Automated backup solutions ensure that critical data is preserved despite hardware failures, software glitches, or unforeseen disasters.

Not all data remains equally valuable over time. Data retention and archiving policies determine how long data is kept and when it should be archived or deleted. Regulatory requirements and business needs often guide these policies. Implementing data retention schedules ensures data is available when needed, while archiving infrequently accessed data helps optimize storage resources.

Data storage and organization practices should encompass data cleaning and quality assurance efforts. Data cleaning involves identifying and rectifying inconsistencies, errors, and duplicates in datasets. Quality assurance ensures that data meets defined accuracy, completeness, and consistency standards. Adequately cleaned and quality-checked data forms the foundation for accurate and reliable insights.

As organizations evolve, data storage needs change. Data migration strategies enable seamless data movement from one storage solution to another while ensuring data integrity. Scalability considerations are essential to accommodate data growth and changing requirements. Organizations should design their storage infrastructure to scale horizontally or vertically, enabling them to handle increased data volumes without compromising performance.

Effective data storage and organization practices promote collaboration and knowledge sharing within organizations. Providing clear documentation about data sources, definitions, and transformations fosters a common understanding among data users. Collaboration platforms and data cataloging tools enable teams to collaborate, share insights, and make informed decisions based on a unified understanding of data.

In the data-driven landscape, best practices for data storage and organization serve as the bedrock for successful data management strategies. Proper data storage infrastructure, classification, metadata management, governance, security measures, and quality assurance contribute to data accessibility, reliability, and value. Effective data organization ensures that insights are derived accurately and efficiently, fostering informed decision-making and innovation. As organizations navigate the complexities of data management, adhering to these best practices will guide them toward optimizing their data assets, unleashing their potential, and driving success in the digital age.

## Ensuring data quality and integrity

In the digital age, where data serves as the foundation of informed decision-making, innovation, and business strategies, ensuring data quality and integrity has become paramount. Data accuracy, reliability, and consistency are essential to derive meaningful insights and actionable outcomes. Organizations prioritizing data quality and integrity are better equipped to make informed decisions, drive competitive advantages, and maintain stakeholder trust.

Data quality and integrity are essential components of effective data management. Poor data quality can lead to flawed analyses, misguided decisions, and ultimately hinder an organization's ability to achieve its goals. Inaccurate or inconsistent data erodes trust in information systems, damages reputation, and affects customer satisfaction. On the other hand, data of high quality and integrity enhances an organization's ability to generate insights that drive strategic decisions, optimize operations, and deliver value to stakeholders. Moreover, in regulated industries such as healthcare and finance, maintaining data integrity is essential for operational excellence and compliance with regulatory standards.

However, numerous challenges accompany the task of ensuring data quality and integrity. Data comes from diverse sources and undergoes various transformations, introducing errors, inconsistencies, and duplications. Lack of standardized data entry practices, human error, and incomplete or outdated information further contribute to poor data quality. Additionally, the complexity of modern data ecosystems, including data lakes, data warehouses, and external data sources, can complicate efforts to maintain consistency and reliability.

To address these challenges, organizations employ a range of best practices. Data profiling involves analyzing datasets to understand their structure, content, and quality. Organizations acquire insights into the quality of their data by identifying anomalies, outliers, and potential errors. Standardizing data entry practices, formats, and values reduces inconsistencies and errors. Validation rules can be implemented to ensure that the data entered meets predefined criteria. Data cleaning involves identifying and rectifying errors, inconsistencies, and duplicates in datasets. This process often requires manual intervention and automated tools to detect and correct discrepancies. Additionally, data transformation involves converting data into a standardized format, making it more suitable for analysis and reporting.

Automated data quality tools have gained prominence, using algorithms and predefined rules to assess data and generate reports highlighting areas that require attention. Data governance establishes the policies, processes, and standards for data management. Data stewards are assigned responsibilities to ensure data quality and integrity. Implementing data governance practices fosters accountability, ownership, and adherence to data quality standards. Metadata management maintains accurate metadata, providing insights into data lineage, transformations, and sources, enabling users to understand data's origins and history.

Regular monitoring and auditing are crucial aspects of maintaining data quality. Organizations establish data quality metrics, conduct regular audits, and address issues promptly to maintain the reliability of their data assets. Furthermore, data quality training and awareness initiatives educate employees about the importance of data quality, fostering a culture that values accurate and reliable data.

Data integrity, which ensures that data remains accurate and unchanged over its lifecycle, is a crucial aspect of data quality. Organizations employ various strategies to maintain data integrity and prevent unauthorized changes or corruption. Implementing access controls and permissions restricts data modification to authorized individuals. Role-based access ensures that only those with appropriate privileges can modify data. Version control and change tracking mechanisms keep a record of data changes over time, allowing organizations to return to previous versions in the event of errors or unauthorized changes.

Using checksums and hashing techniques, organizations can verify data integrity by comparing the original data with a hash value generated from the data. Any changes to the data result in a different hash value, alerting to potential data manipulation. Additionally, data encryption safeguards against unauthorized access and tampering. Encryption ensures that even if data is compromised, it remains unreadable without the appropriate decryption keys. Employing digital signatures enables users to verify the authenticity and integrity of electronic documents, assuring that data has not been altered since the signature was applied.

In conclusion, data quality and integrity are pivotal in the success of organizations in the digital age. Ensuring accurate, reliable, and consistent data is essential for making informed decisions, building trust, and driving innovation. Despite the challenges posed by diverse data sources and complex data ecosystems, organizations can employ a combination of best practices and strategies to maintain data quality and integrity. By embracing data profiling, standardization, automated tools, and governance practices, organizations can overcome hurdles and establish a strong foundation for data-driven success. Strategies such as access controls, encryption, and version control further safeguard data integrity. Ultimately, organizations prioritizing data quality and integrity position themselves for excellence in a data-driven world.

# CHAPTER IV

# Data Preprocessing and Cleaning

## Importance of data preprocessing

In the realm of data science and analytics, the process of data preprocessing stands as a critical precursor to extracting meaningful insights and building accurate models. Data preprocessing encompasses a series of techniques that clean, transform, and refine raw data into a usable format, addressing inconsistencies, errors, and anomalies that can distort analyses and hinder model performance. This section delves into the significance of data preprocessing, exploring its role in enhancing data quality, improving analytical outcomes, and facilitating the development of robust machine learning models.

Data quality is a cornerstone of effective data analysis. Raw data often originates from diverse sources, such as databases, sensors, social media, and external APIs, leading to inherent discrepancies, missing values, and noise. Data preprocessing involves identifying and rectifying these issues to ensure that the data used for analysis is accurate, reliable, and representative of the real world. By cleaning data, filling in missing values, and removing duplicates, data preprocessing creates a solid foundation on which subsequent analyses and modeling can rely. High-quality data yields trustworthy insights, informs decision-making, and prevents incorrect conclusions drawn from erroneous information.

Missing values within datasets are common but can introduce bias and hinder analysis. Data preprocessing techniques, such as imputation, provide solutions for handling missing values. Imputation methods estimate missing values based on the available data, ensuring that analyses are conducted on complete datasets. However, imputation requires careful consideration to avoid distorting the data's underlying distribution or introducing bias. By addressing missing values appropriately, data preprocessing ensures that valuable information is not lost and that analyses reflect a more accurate representation of the phenomenon under study.

Data preprocessing encompasses transformation and scaling techniques that normalize data distributions and bring consistency to variables with differing units or scales. Techniques like normalization and standardization ensure that variables have comparable magnitudes, preventing certain features from dominating the analysis due to their larger scales. Normalized data also aids in improving the performance of machine learning algorithms, which might struggle with unbalanced features. Data transformation techniques enhance the quality of analyses and contribute to the stability and convergence of machine learning models.

Data points known as outliers, which differ dramatically from the average can distort analysis and impair the effectiveness of models. Data preprocessing involves outlier detection and handling methods that identify and manage these anomalies. Techniques such as z-score, IQR (interquartile range), and clustering-based approaches help identify outliers that warrant further investigation or removal. By addressing outliers, data preprocessing ensures that models and analyses are not skewed by extreme values, leading to more accurate and robust results.

In complex datasets, not all features contribute equally to analysis or model performance. Data preprocessing involves feature selection and extraction techniques that identify relevant features and reduce dimensionality. Data preprocessing simplifies analyses and model training by eliminating irrelevant or redundant features, improving efficiency and reducing the risk of overfitting. Feature extraction techniques, like the Principal Component Analysis (PCA), transform original features into a lower-dimensional space while retaining relevant information. This dimensionality reduction enhances model interpretability and performance.

Skewed data distributions, where one class is significantly more prevalent than others, can impact the performance of machine learning algorithms, especially in classification tasks. Data preprocessing techniques include methods to address class imbalance, such as oversampling the minority class or undersampling the majority class. Balancing skewed data ensures that models do not exhibit bias toward the majority class and can provide accurate predictions for all classes. Data preprocessing contributes to fair and equitable modeling outcomes by addressing class imbalance.

In the realm of machine learning, data preprocessing plays a pivotal role in improving model performance. Raw and unprocessed data may contain noise, irrelevant features, or inconsistencies hindering model accuracy and generalization. Data preprocessing techniques prepare the data for model training by ensuring it adheres to machine learning algorithms' assumptions. Cleaned, transformed, and normalized data provides a more stable and reliable foundation for model training, enabling algorithms to learn patterns and relationships more effectively.

In the data-driven era, where insights guide decision-making and innovation, data preprocessing emerges as an indispensable step in the machine learning and data analysis pipelines. Data preprocessing ensures that raw data is refined into a reliable and informative format by enhancing data quality, addressing missing values, handling outliers, and transforming variables. These techniques facilitate accurate analyses and insights and lay the groundwork for robust machine learning models. As organizations continue leveraging data for strategic advantage, recognizing the importance of data preprocessing becomes critical to ensuring the accuracy, reliability, and integrity of their data-driven endeavors.

## Data cleaning techniques: handling missing values, outlier detection, etc.

In data science and analysis, data cleaning is a fundamental step in the data preprocessing pipeline. Raw data, often obtained from various sources, is rarely perfect, and imperfections can lead to inaccurate insights and compromised model performance. Data cleaning techniques encompass a range of methods designed to identify and rectify inconsistencies, errors, and anomalies within datasets. This section delves into the significance of data cleaning, exploring its various techniques, including handling missing values, outlier detection, duplicate removal, and addressing inconsistent data, to ensure that data remains accurate, reliable, and suitable for meaningful analysis.

Missing values are a common occurrence in datasets, stemming from various factors such as data collection errors, sensor malfunctions, or intentional omissions. However, the presence of missing values can introduce bias and inaccuracies into analyses and models. Data cleaning involves employing techniques to handle missing values, ensuring that the analysis is conducted on complete datasets. Imputation, a prevalent approach, involves estimating missing values based on the available data. Common imputation methods include mean imputation, median imputation, and regression imputation. While imputation can provide usable data, it's crucial to consider the implications of imputed values on the analysis and model outcomes, as improper imputation can lead to distorted results.

Data points that substantially depart from the dataset's overall pattern are called outliers. They can arise from measurement errors, rare events, or genuine anomalies. If not addressed, outliers can distort analyses and lead to erroneous conclusions. Data cleaning includes techniques for detecting and managing outliers. Statistical methods like the z-score and the interquartile range (IQR) can help identify outliers by measuring the data's deviation from the mean or quartiles. Once identified, outliers can be handled through various methods, such as removal, transformation, or imputation. Handling outliers ensures that the data used for analysis is representative of the underlying patterns and relationships within the dataset.

Duplicate records within datasets can skew analyses and lead to incorrect insights. Data cleaning involves identifying and removing duplicate entries to maintain data consistency and accuracy. Duplicate detection methods compare records based on their attributes, identifying records with identical or very similar values. Upon detection, organizations can choose to retain one instance of the duplicate records or remove all duplicates, ensuring that each data point contributes meaningfully to the analysis.

Inconsistent data formatting can arise from variations in data entry practices, units of measurement, or categorization. Data cleaning techniques include standardization and transformation methods that unify data formats, making them suitable for analysis. For example, converting date formats to a common standard or converting measurements to a consistent unit ensures that analyses are conducted on standardized data. Inconsistent data can lead to calculation errors, incorrect visualizations, and hindered model performance. By addressing data inconsistencies, data cleaning facilitates accurate analysis and modeling.

Data cleaning plays a crucial role in improving the performance of machine learning models. Raw data often contains noise, irrelevant features, or inconsistencies hindering model accuracy and generalization. By employing data cleaning techniques, machine learning practitioners ensure that the data used for model training adheres to the assumptions of the chosen algorithms. Cleaned and preprocessed data provides a more stable foundation for model training, enabling algorithms to learn patterns and relationships more effectively. Data cleaning not only improves model performance but also prevents models from learning spurious associations or patterns introduced by inconsistencies in the data.

While data cleaning techniques offer substantial benefits, they also present challenges that practitioners must navigate. Imputation, for instance, involves making educated guesses about missing values, which can introduce biases if not handled carefully. Similarly, outlier detection may lead to the removal of valid data points that contribute to understanding rare phenomena.

Striking a balance between data preservation and enhancing data quality is crucial. Additionally, the choice of data cleaning techniques should be context-specific, considering the nature of the data, the objectives of analysis, and the intended use of the cleaned data.

In the data-driven landscape, where informed decisions and accurate insights are paramount, data cleaning techniques emerge as indispensable processes in the data preprocessing journey. By addressing missing values, detecting outliers, removing duplicates, and standardizing data formats, data cleaning ensures that data remains accurate, reliable, and suitable for meaningful analysis. These techniques not only enhance data quality but also enhance the performance of machine learning models by providing a stable foundation for training. As organizations continue to leverage data for strategic advantage, recognizing the significance of data cleaning becomes pivotal to ensuring accurate, reliable, and insightful analyses that drive innovation and success in the digital age.


## Data transformation and feature engineering

In data science and machine learning, data transformation and feature engineering are essential techniques that elevate raw data into actionable insights and predictive models. These processes involve manipulating and creating new features from existing data, enabling algorithms to uncover patterns, relationships, and trends that might otherwise remain hidden. This section explores the significance of data transformation and feature engineering, delving into their roles in enhancing model performance, enabling domain- specific insights, and driving innovation across diverse industries.

Data transformation encompasses a series of techniques that modify, scale, or reshape data to improve its suitability for analysis and modeling. Raw data often arrives in various formats, units, and scales, hindering accurate analyses and model convergence. Transformation techniques, such as normalization, standardization, and log transformations, bring data distributions to consistent scales, reducing the impact of features with larger magnitudes and ensuring that algorithms perform optimally. These transformations enhance model performance and aid in visualizations, facilitating a clearer understanding of data patterns and relationships.

Feature engineering entails creating new features from existing data or domain knowledge to enhance the performance of machine learning models. Raw data may not contain explicit information relevant to the problem at hand, but domain expertise can be incorporated through feature engineering to extract relevant insights. For example, in natural language processing, features like word frequencies or sentiment scores can be engineered from text data to capture underlying sentiments or topics. Feature engineering enables models to capture complex relationships and nuances in the data, improving their predictive power.

Data transformation and feature engineering play a crucial role in capturing nonlinear relationships within the data. Linear models might struggle to capture intricate patterns in data that exhibit nonlinear dependencies. Techniques like polynomial transformations, interaction terms, and binning can introduce nonlinearities into the data, allowing models to capture complex interactions better. Feature engineering goes beyond linear relationships, enabling models to uncover intricate and context-specific patterns influencing outcomes.

Feature engineering empowers organizations to leverage domain-specific insights that are not evident from raw data alone. In medical diagnostics, for instance, features related to patient history, demographics, and medical records can be engineered to enhance the accuracy of disease prediction models. Similarly, in financial fraud detection, features related to transaction behavior, user profiles, and transaction timestamps can provide crucial information for accurate fraud detection. By incorporating domain knowledge, feature engineering ensures that models capture nuances that are vital for precise predictions and decisions.

In many real-world applications, datasets are characterized by many features. High-dimensional data can lead to overfitting, increased computational costs, and reduced model interpretability. Feature engineering techniques, such as dimensionality reduction, help mitigate these challenges. Methods like Principal Component Analysis (or PCA) and t-Distributed Stochastic Neighbor Embedding (or t-SNE) reduce the number of features while retaining essential information. Dimensionality reduction simplifies models, accelerates training times, and enhances model generalization.

While data transformation and feature engineering offer immense benefits, they also present challenges that require careful consideration. Overengineering features, creating irrelevant attributes, or introducing biases can lead to poor model performance or incorrect insights. It's essential to strike a balance between adding meaningful features and preventing model complexity. Domain expertise is crucial, as understanding the data and its relationships enables practitioners to engineer features that are relevant and aligned with the problem's context.

Data transformation and feature engineering represent a blend of scientific rigor and creative artistry. Practitioners need to possess technical skills and an understanding of the problem domain. Experimentation and iteration play a significant role, as different transformations and engineered features might yield varying results. Exploratory data analysis, visualization, and domain knowledge guide selecting appropriate techniques and features that uncover insights and enhance model performance.

The impact of data transformation and feature engineering is felt across industries. In healthcare, these techniques enhance disease prediction models, aiding clinicians in making timely and accurate diagnoses. In finance, they power fraud detection algorithms that safeguard transactions and customer accounts. In marketing, feature engineering enables personalized recommendations, elevating customer engagement. The applications span across domains, driving innovation and transformation in diverse sectors.

Data transformation and feature engineering are the cornerstones of extracting insights and creating effective predictive models from raw data. By transforming data distributions, introducing nonlinearities, and crafting domain-specific features, practitioners unlock the potential of data to reveal hidden patterns and relationships. The marriage of technical expertise and domain knowledge fuels the process, enabling organizations to build models that accurately predict outcomes, inform decisions, and drive innovation. In the always changing landscape of data science and machine learning, data transformation and feature engineering are potent techniques that bridge the gap between data and insights, paving the way for a future powered by data-driven excellence.

## Tools and libraries for data preprocessing

In data science and analytics, the journey from raw data to actionable insights is paved by a series of essential steps, with data preprocessing playing a pivotal role. Data preprocessing involves cleaning, transforming, and refining raw data to make it suitable for analysis and modeling. To accomplish this, data professionals rely on various tools and libraries that streamline the data preprocessing process, enabling efficient data transformation and feature engineering. This section delves into the significance of tools and libraries for data preprocessing, exploring their functionalities, advantages, and role in accelerating data-driven decision-making and innovation.

Python, a versatile and widely used programming language, offers a plethora of libraries that excel in data preprocessing tasks. Pandas is one of the most prominent tools, providing data structures and functions for effectively manipulating and analyzing data. Pandas' DataFrame and Series structures enable users to easily handle missing values, remove duplicates, and perform data transformations. Moreover, the library offers powerful functionalities for data aggregation, grouping, and merging, facilitating complex data preprocessing tasks.

NumPy, another foundational Python library, focuses on numerical operations and array manipulation. It is the backbone for many other libraries and tools in the data preprocessing ecosystem. NumPy arrays enable efficient vectorized operations, simplifying tasks like data transformation, computation of summary statistics, and mathematical operations on large datasets. NumPy's seamless integration with Pandas and other libraries further enhances its role in data preprocessing workflows.

Data preprocessing is often intertwined with machine learning tasks, and scikit-learn, a comprehensive machine learning library, offers robust preprocessing functionalities. The library provides preprocessing modules that handle scaling, encoding categorical variables, and feature selection tasks. Scikit-learn's integration with machine learning algorithms ensures that data preprocessing seamlessly integrates into the model development pipeline, improving model performance and generalization.

Feature engineering, a critical aspect of data preprocessing, benefits from specialized libraries like feature-engine. This library offers a wide array of techniques for feature transformation, imputation, and handling categorical variables. Feature-engine's modular design allows practitioners to tailor their feature engineering strategies to the specific needs of their datasets and models, enhancing the quality and predictive power of engineered features.

DataRobot, an automated machine learning platform, extends its capabilities to data preprocessing. The platform offers automated data cleansing, imputation, and transformation, streamlining the process of getting data ready for analysis and modeling. DataRobot's automated approach reduces manual effort, accelerates preprocessing tasks, and ensures consistent and standardized data preprocessing across projects.

OpenRefine, an open-source tool, cleans and transforms messy and inconsistent data. It provides a user-friendly interface for exploring, refining, and transforming data using a range of operations such as clustering, filtering, and editing. OpenRefine is particularly valuable for preprocessing tasks involving diverse and unstructured data sources, making data cleaning and transformation accessible to individuals without extensive programming skills.

KNIME, an open-source data analytics platform, offers a visual interface for designing data preprocessing workflows. Users can drag and drop nodes to perform data cleaning, transformation, and enrichment tasks. KNIME's visual approach enables easy experimentation, collaboration, and iteration in data preprocessing, making it suitable for both novices and experts.

Trifacta focuses on data wrangling, which involves cleaning, transforming, and enriching data for analysis. Its user-friendly interface empowers data professionals to explore, clean, and transform data by utilizing a visual interface. Trifacta's machine learning-driven suggestions enhance efficiency, enabling users to uncover patterns and insights in the data while preparing it for analysis.

Utilizing specialized tools and libraries for data preprocessing offers numerous advantages that streamline workflows and enhance productivity. Automation reduces manual effort and accelerates preprocessing tasks, enabling data professionals to focus on higher-level analysis and decision-making. Consistent and standardized preprocessing, facilitated by these tools, ensures reproducibility and consistency across projects. Moreover, these tools' wide range of functionalities caters to various data preprocessing needs, from simple cleaning tasks to complex feature engineering.

While tools and libraries offer substantial benefits, their usage comes with considerations and challenges. Selecting the appropriate tool or library depends on factors such as the nature of the data, the complexity of preprocessing tasks, and the expertise of the users. Learning curve and compatibility with existing workflows are important factors to consider. Customization and fine-tuning may also be necessary to adapt these tools to specific data preprocessing requirements.

Tools and libraries emerge as indispensable allies in the data-driven landscape, where the quality of insights and models hinges on effective data preprocessing. Python, scikit-learn, feature-engine, and more empower data professionals to handle missing values efficiently, transform data distributions, engineer features, and streamline preprocessing workflows. Specialized tools like DataRobot, OpenRefine, KNIME, and Trifacta further enhance automation, collaboration, and exploration in data preprocessing. As organizations continue to harness the power of data for innovation and strategic decision-making, recognizing the significance of these tools and libraries becomes pivotal in ensuring accurate, reliable, and impactful data preprocessing that drives excellence in the digital age.

# CHAPTER V

# Exploratory Data Analysis (EDA)

## Purpose of EDA in big data analysis

In the era of big data, where organizations amass vast volumes of information from diverse sources, the role of data analysis has never been more critical. Amid this data deluge, the process of Exploratory Data Analysis (EDA) emerges as a fundamental step in deriving meaningful insights, patterns, and trends from the vast and complex datasets characteristic of big data. This section delves into the purpose of EDA in big data analysis, elucidating its significance in understanding data characteristics, identifying anomalies, guiding further analyses, and facilitating data-driven decision-making across diverse industries.

In the world of big data, where data streams in from many sources, EDA serves as a gateway to unravel the stories hidden within the data. EDA involves visualizing and summarizing data to comprehend its characteristics, distributions, and relationships. In big data analysis, where datasets can span multiple dimensions and features, EDA provides a means to grasp the data's essence without being overwhelmed by its sheer size. By plotting histograms, scatter plots, and box plots, analysts gain insights into data distributions, outliers, and patterns that serve as the foundation for further investigation and analysis.

Big data often encompasses noise, inconsistencies, and anomalies that can distort analyses and impact decision-making. EDA plays a pivotal role in identifying these anomalies and outliers that deviate from the expected patterns. Data professionals can spot irregularities that warrant further investigation through visualizations and statistical techniques. In sectors like finance and healthcare, where anomalies can have significant consequences, EDA becomes a crucial tool for ensuring data quality and maintaining the integrity of analyses.

In big data, where the potential for analysis is boundless, EDA serves as a compass that guides subsequent analyses. By uncovering relationships, dependencies, and trends, EDA informs the selection of appropriate analysis techniques and models. Visualizations from EDA might indicate correlations that prompt regression analysis, clustering tendencies that suggest segmentation, or temporal patterns that inspire time-series analysis. EDA ensures that the chosen analyses are not based on assumptions but are grounded in the observed data characteristics, leading to more accurate and insightful results.

Visualizing big data is a formidable challenge due to its size and complexity. EDA addresses this challenge by offering visualization techniques that provide a glimpse into the multidimensional nature of big data. Heatmaps, scatter plots, and interactive visualizations allow analysts to explore data from various angles and dimensions, aiding in pattern recognition and hypothesis generation. Visualization is a powerful means to communicate insights to stakeholders, enabling them to grasp complex information at a glance.

EDA in big data analysis often involves collaboration between data professionals and domain experts. The amalgamation of domain knowledge and EDA results can lead to hypothesis generation that drives focused analyses. For instance, a combination of clinical expertise and EDA might reveal potential correlations between patient characteristics and disease outcomes in healthcare. In marketing, EDA might uncover consumer behavior patterns that can guide targeted campaigns when combined with industry knowledge. The iterative process of hypothesis generation and testing harnesses the potential of big data to derive actionable insights.

In big data, dimensionality can be overwhelming, making it challenging to discern patterns and relationships. EDA aids in reducing dimensionality by highlighting important features and relationships. Techniques like dimensionality reduction, facilitated by methods like Principal Component Analysis (PCA), transform high-dimensional data into lower-dimensional representations. EDA guides the selection of relevant features that capture the essence of the data, enhancing the efficiency of subsequent analyses and modeling.

Ethical considerations come to the forefront as big data analysis impacts decision-making across domains. EDA plays a role in promoting transparency and fairness in analyses. By visualizing data distributions, biases, and potential disparities, EDA uncovers potential ethical concerns about representation, diversity, and equity. This awareness enables data professionals to address biases, validate findings, and ensure that decisions based on big data are ethically sound.

While EDA is invaluable in big data analysis, it faces challenges related to scalability and visualization. Traditional EDA techniques might struggle to handle large datasets due to computational limitations. Advanced visualization tools and techniques that leverage parallel processing and sampling become crucial in visualizing big data. Moreover, crafting meaningful visualizations that convey insights from high-dimensional data demands creativity and expertise, as displaying multiple dimensions in two dimensions is inherently challenging.

In big data analysis, Exploratory Data Analysis (EDA) emerges as a beacon that guides data professionals through the vast and complex information landscape. By uncovering data characteristics, identifying anomalies, and guiding subsequent analyses, EDA empowers organizations to extract actionable insights from the wealth of data at their disposal. The marriage of visualizations, statistical techniques, and domain expertise transforms raw data into a canvas that reveals hidden patterns, informs decision-making, and fuels innovation. In the era where data is hailed as the new oil, EDA is the compass that navigates through this sea of information, illuminating pathways to knowledge, progress, and success across industries and domains.

## Visualization techniques for understanding data distributions

In the realm of data analysis and interpretation, the ability to grasp the underlying distribution of data is paramount. Visualization techniques are powerful for unraveling complex data distributions, enabling data professionals to gain insights, detect patterns, and make informed decisions. This section delves into the significance of visualization techniques for understanding data distributions, exploring various methods such as histograms, density plots, box plots, violin plots, and probability plots. By illuminating the intricacies of data distributions, these visualization techniques empower analysts to extract meaningful information and guide data-driven endeavors across diverse domains.

Histograms are one of the most fundamental visualization techniques for understanding data distributions. They visually represent the frequency or count of data points within predefined bins or intervals. By plotting data on the x-axis and frequency on the y-axis, histograms offer insights into data distributions' shape, spread, and central tendency. Histograms enable analysts to identify modes, detect skewness, and uncover potential outliers, facilitating a holistic understanding of how data points are distributed across different ranges.

Density plots, also known as kernel density plots, complement histograms by providing a continuous estimate of the data distribution's underlying probability density function. These plots offer a smoothed representation of the data distribution, emphasizing patterns and trends while minimizing the impact of random fluctuations that can occur in histograms. Density plots offer insights into the shape of the distribution, highlighting multimodality, skewness, and concentration of data points. The smoothness of density plots makes them particularly useful for visualizing continuous data distributions.

Box plots, or box-and-whisker plots, offer a concise yet powerful visualization of data distributions. They display the median, quartiles, and potential outliers within a dataset. Box plots allow analysts to identify the central tendency and spread of data and detect skewness or asymmetry. Additionally, they offer insights into potential outliers that might deviate significantly from the rest of the data. Box plots are especially valuable when comparing data distributions across different groups or categories, enabling visual comparisons of medians and ranges.

Violin plots combine the benefits of density plots and box plots, providing a comprehensive view of data distributions. These plots showcase the density estimation of the data distribution on either side of a central box plot, resembling the shape of a violin. By integrating the smoothness of density plots with the summary statistics of box plots, violin plots offer a rich visualization encompassing data distribution characteristics, multimodality, and presence of outliers. Violin plots are particularly effective when conveying complex distributions or when comparing distributions across multiple categories.

Probability plots, also known as Q-Q (quantile-quantile) plots, provide a valuable tool for assessing the distributional fit of data to a theoretical distribution, often the normal distribution. These plots compare the quantiles of the dataset against the quantiles of the theoretical distribution, generating a scatter plot along a diagonal line if the data is normally distributed. Deviations from the diagonal indicate departures from normality, enabling analysts to make informed decisions about data transformations, model assumptions, and the appropriateness of statistical tests.

Visualization techniques for understanding data distributions find applications across diverse industries and domains. In finance, these techniques enable analysts to assess the distribution of financial returns, aiding in risk assessment and portfolio management. In healthcare, they facilitate the analysis of patient outcomes and medical test results, guiding medical decisions. In marketing, understanding customer purchase patterns and preferences helps tailor marketing strategies. The applications span from scientific research to social sciences, from manufacturing to entertainment, underscoring the universal relevance of these visualization techniques.

With the advent of interactive visualization tools, analysts can now explore data distributions in dynamic and interactive ways. Tools like Tableau, Plotly, and D3.js enable users to interact with visualizations, zooming in on specific data ranges, hovering over data points for details, and filtering data subsets for deeper insights. Interactive visualization enhances the exploratory process, enabling data professionals to uncover patterns and anomalies that might remain hidden in static plots. Moreover, these tools facilitate communication of insights to stakeholders, fostering a better understanding of data distributions and their implications.

While visualization techniques offer valuable insights, challenges in interpretation and choice of visualization method persist. Selecting the right technique depends on the nature of the data, its distributional characteristics, and the insights sought. Complex data distributions might demand combining techniques to convey the complete picture. Moreover, misinterpretation of visualizations can lead to incorrect conclusions. A skewed plot might be mistaken for normality, or outliers might be overlooked if not identified appropriately. Thus, a thorough understanding of visualization techniques and their implications is essential for accurate interpretation.

In the data-driven era, where insights guide decisions and innovation, visualization techniques for understanding data distributions emerge as essential tools for data professionals. Histograms, density plots, box plots, violin plots, and probability plots provide a canvas that unveils the intricacies of data distributions. By offering insights into shape, central tendency, spread, and potential anomalies, these techniques empower analysts to comprehend data characteristics, identify patterns, and make informed decisions. The ability to visualize data distributions transcends industries, domains, and disciplines, making these techniques a cornerstone of exploratory data analysis and a catalyst for transformative discoveries in the dynamic landscape of data science.

## Uncovering patterns, correlations, and anomalies

In the vast landscape of data science and analysis, extracting meaningful insights from complex datasets is a pivotal challenge. Uncovering patterns, correlations, and anomalies within data not only aids in understanding underlying relationships but also drives informed decision-making and innovation across diverse domains. This section delves into the significance of uncovering patterns, correlations, and anomalies in data analysis, exploring methods such as correlation analysis, clustering techniques, and anomaly detection. By navigating through the depths of data, these techniques empower data professionals to unravel hidden insights, glean actionable information, and propel progress in the ever- evolving world of data-driven discovery.

Correlation analysis emerges as a foundational technique for uncovering relationships between variables. It quantifies the strength and direction of linear relationships between pairs of variables. Pearson correlation coefficient, Spearman rank correlation, and also Kendall tau rank correlation are common methods for quantifying correlations. A high positive correlation indicates that as one variable increases, the other tends to increase as well, while a high negative correlation suggests an inverse relationship. Correlation analysis is essential for identifying potential cause-and-effect relationships, guiding feature selection for modeling, and validating hypotheses in various domains.

Cluster analysis, a powerful unsupervised learning technique, enables grouping data points into clusters that is based on their similarities. Clusters represent subsets of data points that share common characteristics. Techniques like k-means clustering and hierarchical clustering group data based on distances or similarities between observations. Cluster analysis is instrumental in segmenting customers based on purchasing behavior, identifying distinct patterns in biological data, and classifying textual data into thematic groups. By grouping similar data points, cluster analysis uncovers patterns and structures that might not be apparent through individual data point examination.

Uncovering patterns in high-dimensional data can be challenging due to the "curse of dimensionality." Principal Component Analysis, also known as PCA, a dimensionality reduction technique, addresses this challenge by transforming high-dimensional data into a lower-dimensional representation while retaining the maximum variance. PCA identifies orthogonal axes, known as principal components, that capture the most important variations in the data. These components reveal dominant patterns and relationships, enabling analysts to visualize data in a reduced-dimensional space and identify key features that drive variance. PCA facilitates data visualization, model simplification, and a deeper understanding of complex data patterns.

Time-series data, characterized by sequential measurements over time, demands specialized techniques for pattern discovery. Time-series analysis encompasses methods like moving averages, exponential smoothing, and autoregressive integrated moving average (or ARIMA) models. These techniques unveil temporal patterns, trends, and seasonality within data. Time-series analysis is crucial in finance for forecasting stock prices, epidemiology for tracking disease outbreaks, and climate science for predicting weather patterns. By capturing time-dependent patterns, this analysis aids in making predictions, optimizing resource allocation, and understanding the dynamics of evolving phenomena.

Anomalies, or outliers, are data points that significantly deviate from the expected patterns within a dataset. Anomaly detection techniques aim to identify these deviations, which could indicate errors, fraud, or rare events. Statistical methods, clustering-based approaches, and machine learning algorithms can uncover anomalies. In finance, anomaly detection helps in fraud prevention by identifying unusual transactions. In manufacturing, it aids in quality control by flagging defective products. By pinpointing anomalies, these techniques enable organizations to address potential issues, ensure data integrity, and make informed decisions.

Text data, abundant in various forms, holds valuable insights for analysis. Text mining and natural language processing (or NLP) techniques uncover patterns and relationships within textual data. Sentiment analysis detects sentiments and emotions from text, aiding in understanding customer feedback and opinions. Topic modeling identifies underlying themes in large text corpora, enabling categorization and summarization. Named entity recognition extracts entities like names, dates, and locations from text, facilitating information extraction. In the digital age, text mining and NLP are pivotal in analyzing social media content, news articles, and customer reviews, guiding sentiment analysis, trend detection, and brand perception analysis.

While uncovering patterns, correlations, and anomalies is essential for data-driven insights, interpretation, noise, and bias challenges persist. Spurious correlations might arise from coincidental relationships or omitted variables. Overfitting, a common challenge, occurs when models capture noise instead of true patterns. Contextual understanding is crucial; a correlation between variables might not imply causation. Moreover, the choice of techniques depends on the nature of data and the specific objectives of analysis. For example, clustering might result in different groupings depending on the algorithm chosen.

In the dynamic landscape of data science, the ability to uncover patterns, correlations, and anomalies represents a cornerstone of knowledge discovery and decision-making. From identifying causal relationships through correlation analysis to grouping similar data points using cluster analysis, data professionals traverse a diverse toolkit to uncover insights that inform strategies and actions. Whether through the lens of dimensionality reduction, time-series analysis, or anomaly detection, the pursuit of pattern recognition and anomaly identification underpins innovation across industries. As the digital universe continues to expand, these techniques shine as guiding lights, illuminating the path to understanding, foresight, and transformative impact through the power of data.

# Case studies showcasing effective EDA

Exploratory Data Analysis (EDA) serves as a cornerstone in the realm of data science, enabling analysts to uncover hidden insights, patterns, and trends within complex datasets. Real-world case studies provide tangible examples of how EDA can transform raw data into actionable insights, driving decision-making and innovation across diverse domains. This section delves into case studies showcasing effective EDA, exploring instances where EDA has unveiled meaningful patterns, guided strategies, and informed critical decisions. By examining these real-world examples, we illuminate the transformative potential of EDA in harnessing the power of data for a wide range of applications.

*Case Study 1: Detecting Disease Outbreaks Through Temporal Analysis*

In the field of epidemiology, EDA plays a pivotal role in detecting disease outbreaks and understanding their dynamics. A notable case study involves using EDA to analyze the spread of the Zika virus. Researchers analyzed time-series data of reported Zika cases and temperature trends in affected regions. By visualizing the temporal patterns and correlations between cases and temperature fluctuations, they identified a potential link between rising temperatures and increased Zika infections. This discovery guided public health interventions, enabling timely responses to outbreaks and highlighting the importance of climate-sensitive disease surveillance.

*Case Study 2: Uncovering Consumer Behavior Patterns for Retail Strategy*

In the realm of retail, EDA guides strategies by uncovering consumer behavior patterns from transactional data. A case study involving a global e-commerce platform exemplifies this. Analysts conducted EDA on customer purchase history, identifying recurrent purchasing patterns and clusters of similar buying behavior. This insight enabled the platform to personalize recommendations, optimize inventory management, and design targeted marketing campaigns. By leveraging EDA, the e-commerce giant enhanced customer engagement, improved sales conversion rates, and strengthened customer loyalty through data-driven insights.

*Case Study 3: Enhancing Financial Fraud Detection*

Financial institutions harness EDA to combat fraud by identifying abnormal transactions and patterns indicative of fraudulent activities. A case study involving a credit card company showcases the effectiveness of EDA in fraud detection. Analysts explored transaction data, visualizing spending patterns, transaction frequencies, and geographical locations. Through EDA, they identified unusual spending behavior, uncovering instances of unauthorized transactions. This information empowered the company to promptly block compromised cards, mitigate losses, and reinforce fraud prevention mechanisms.

*Case Study 4: Optimizing Supply Chain Operations*

Effective supply chain management relies on understanding demand patterns, inventory levels, and supplier performance. EDA aids in optimizing these operations by revealing insights from supply chain data. A case study in the manufacturing industry illustrates this impact. Analysts conducted EDA on historical production and inventory data, identifying seasonal demand patterns and inventory shortages. This information facilitated informed procurement decisions, enabling the company to adjust production schedules, avoid stockouts, and minimize excess inventory, ultimately reducing operational costs and improving customer satisfaction.

## Case Study 5: Personalizing Healthcare Interventions

Healthcare providers leverage EDA to personalize interventions and enhance patient outcomes. A case study involving diabetes management demonstrates this application. Researchers analyzed patient data, including medical history, demographics, and treatment adherence. Through EDA, they identified correlations between patient characteristics and treatment effectiveness. This insight informed the design of personalized care plans, enabling healthcare professionals to tailor interventions based on patient profiles. EDA-driven personalized interventions led to improved treatment outcomes and enhanced patient engagement.

## Case Study 6: Guiding Urban Planning Through Spatial Analysis

Urban planning benefits from EDA by extracting insights from spatial data to inform city development strategies. A case study in urban mobility illustrates this impact. Analysts examined geospatial data from rideshare services and public transportation. They visualized traffic patterns, congestion hotspots, and travel behavior through EDA. This information guided urban planners in designing efficient transportation routes, optimizing traffic flow, and improving accessibility for residents. EDA-driven insights fostered sustainable urban development and enhanced quality of life for city dwellers.

These case studies underscore the transformative role of EDA in various domains. They highlight the significance of understanding data distributions, identifying anomalies, and uncovering relationships through visual exploration. Lessons learned from these examples emphasize the iterative nature of EDA, where data professionals continuously refine their analyses based on insights revealed during the exploratory phase. Furthermore, these case studies showcase the interdisciplinary nature of EDA, where domain expertise collaborates with data analysis techniques to generate actionable insights.

While case studies demonstrate the power of EDA, challenges such as bias, data quality, and interpretational pitfalls should not be overlooked. Biased data might lead to skewed insights, and poor data quality might hinder accurate analyses. Interpretation of EDA results requires caution to avoid overgeneralization or misinterpretation of patterns. Contextual understanding is essential to discern correlations from causation and to ensure that EDA-driven decisions align with broader objectives.

The case studies presented illuminate the transformative potential of Exploratory Data Analysis (EDA) across a spectrum of industries and applications. From epidemiology to retail, finance to healthcare, urban planning to supply chain management, EDA serves as a compass that guides organizations through data complexities, unearths hidden insights, and fosters informed decision-making. These real-world examples demonstrate how EDA empowers data professionals to go beyond the surface of data, unveiling patterns, correlations, and anomalies that propel progress and innovation. As the data-driven era continues to evolve, the lessons gleaned from these case studies serve as a testament to EDA's enduring relevance and impact in shaping a future guided by insights, knowledge, and data- driven excellence.

# CHAPTER VI

# Big Data Analytics Techniques

## Introduction to various big data analytics techniques

In the era of big data, where information is generated at an unprecedented pace and scale, traditional data analysis methods prove insufficient to glean meaningful insights from the vast and complex datasets. This prompts the need for advanced analytics techniques tailored to handle the intricacies of big data. This section introduces various big data analytics techniques, exploring methods such as machine learning, natural language processing, network analysis, sentiment analysis, and predictive modeling. By navigating through this landscape of insight generation, we uncover how these techniques empower organizations to extract actionable insights, predict trends, and drive informed decision-making across diverse domains.

Machine learning stands at the forefront of big data analytics, harnessing the power of algorithms to identify patterns, make predictions, and automate decision-making. Supervised learning involves training models on labeled data to predict unseen data points. Unsupervised learning uncovers hidden structures within data through clustering and dimensionality reduction. Semi-supervised learning combines labeled and unlabeled data, and reinforcement learning guides agents to take actions to maximize rewards. Machine learning algorithms like the decision trees, support vector machines, and also neural networks are applied to tasks such as image recognition, fraud detection, customer segmentation, and recommendation systems.

In the digital age, textual data abounds, making Natural Language Processing (NLP) an invaluable tool for deriving insights from unstructured text. NLP techniques enable machines to understand, interpret, and generate human language. Sentiment analysis gauges the sentiment expressed in text, aiding in brand perception analysis and customer feedback assessment. Named entity recognition extracts entities like names, dates, and locations from text, facilitating information extraction. Topic modeling uncovers themes and patterns within large text corpora. NLP's applications span sentiment analysis in social media, summarization of news articles, and automated chatbots for customer service.

Network analysis examines relationships between entities to uncover insights into interconnected systems. In social networks, it reveals influencer dynamics, community structures, and information diffusion. In supply chain networks, it identifies bottlenecks and vulnerabilities. Techniques like centrality measures identify influential nodes, while community detection identifies clusters of related entities. Network analysis helps optimize transportation routes, predict disease spread in epidemiology, and enhance cybersecurity by identifying vulnerable points in computer networks.

Sentiment analysis, a subset of NLP, focuses on understanding and classifying emotions expressed in text. Organizations gain insights into customer opinions, brand perception, and market trends by analyzing sentiment. Sentiment analysis techniques categorize text as positive, negative, or neutral, enabling organizations to assess consumer feedback, track sentiment shifts over time, and adjust marketing strategies accordingly. In the age of social media, sentiment analysis provides real-time insights into public sentiment, guiding crisis management and sentiment-based trading strategies.

Predictive modeling leverages historical data to make informed predictions about future outcomes. This technique aids in forecasting trends, optimizing resources, and making proactive decisions. Regression analysis models relationships between variables to predict continuous outcomes, while classification models categorize data into predefined classes. Time-series forecasting predicts values over time, guiding inventory management, energy consumption estimation, and financial market predictions. Predictive modeling finds applications in predicting customer churn, disease outbreaks, stock prices, and equipment failures.

While big data analytics techniques offer remarkable insights, they come with challenges that demand attention. Data quality and bias impact the accuracy of results. Scalability becomes crucial when applying techniques to massive datasets. Interpreting complex models can be challenging, as they might lack transparency. Ethical considerations arise in cases like bias in predictive models and privacy concerns in NLP. A thorough understanding of the techniques, context, and potential limitations is essential for effective application.

As organizations amass unprecedented volumes of data, harnessing its potential requires specialized big data analytics techniques. Machine learning empowers data-driven decision-making through prediction and automation. Natural Language Processing decodes textual insights, enabling sentiment analysis and information extraction. Network analysis illuminates relationships in interconnected systems, aiding in optimization and security. Sentiment analysis gauges emotional trends, guiding brand strategies and crisis management. Predictive modeling forecasts future outcomes, facilitating proactive strategies. Through these techniques, organizations extract insights and unlock the power of data to predict trends, enhance customer experiences, optimize operations, and drive innovation across industries and domains. As the world embraces the era of big data, applying these techniques will continue to shape a future guided by insights, knowledge, and data-driven excellence.

## Descriptive, diagnostic, predictive, and prescriptive analytics

In the age of data-driven decision-making, organizations rely on a spectrum of analytics techniques to extract insights, guide strategies, and optimize operations. Four key types of analytics—descriptive, diagnostic, predictive, and prescriptive—form the foundation of this endeavor. This section delves into the layers of data insight these analytics types provide, exploring how they transform raw data into actionable intelligence and foster a holistic approach to decision-making across diverse industries and domains.

Descriptive analytics serves as the starting point in the analytics journey, focusing on summarizing historical data to provide an overview of past events and trends. Through data aggregation, visualization, and reporting techniques, descriptive analytics answers the question "What happened?" It transforms raw data into understandable narratives, charts, and graphs that clearly understand historical performance. Descriptive analytics aids in monitoring key performance indicators

(KPIs), assessing trends over time, and providing a snapshot of organizational activities. For instance, in retail, descriptive analytics might reveal sales figures, customer counts, and product preferences, enabling stakeholders to assess past performance and make informed decisions based on historical data.

Moving beyond the "What" of descriptive analytics, diagnostic analytics focuses on uncovering the "Why" behind observed patterns and trends. It delves deeper into the data to identify causal relationships and root causes of events. Techniques such as drill-down analysis, root cause analysis, and hypothesis testing aid in identifying factors that influenced historical outcomes. Organizations gain insights into what led to particular events by understanding the factors driving performance. For instance, diagnostic analytics might reveal that a decrease in customer satisfaction scores was caused by a recent change in product quality, enabling organizations to address the underlying issue and make corrective actions.

Predictive analytics leaps forward by forecasting future outcomes based on historical data and patterns. It employs statistical models and machine learning algorithms to identify trends and predict future events. By answering the question "What is likely to happen?" predictive analytics enables organizations to anticipate future scenarios and take proactive measures. In finance, predictive analytics might be used to forecast stock prices, aiding in investment decisions. In healthcare, it might predict disease outbreaks, enabling timely interventions. By analyzing historical data, predictive analytics empowers organizations to make informed choices, optimize resource allocation, and plan for various contingencies.

Prescriptive analytics represents the pinnacle of the analytics hierarchy, aiming to guide optimal decision-making by providing actionable recommendations. It considers the insights gained from descriptive, diagnostic, and predictive analytics to suggest courses of action that lead to desired outcomes. Techniques like optimization, simulation, and decision trees assist in identifying the best options in complex decision scenarios. Prescriptive analytics answers the question "What should we do?" For example, in supply chain management, prescriptive analytics might recommend inventory levels, production schedules, and distribution routes to minimize costs and maximize efficiency. By providing actionable insights, prescriptive analytics enables organizations to anticipate outcomes and make strategic choices that align with their goals.

While each type of analytics—descriptive, diagnostic, predictive, and prescriptive—offers unique insights, their true power lies in their integration. By leveraging a combination of these analytics types, organizations can foster a holistic approach to decision-making. Descriptive analytics provides context by summarizing historical data, diagnostic analytics uncovers underlying causes, predictive analytics forecasts potential outcomes, and prescriptive analytics guides optimized actions. This integration facilitates a comprehensive understanding of complex scenarios, enabling organizations to make informed decisions that consider past, present, and future factors.

The applicability of these analytics types transcends industries and domains. In manufacturing, descriptive analytics might provide insights into production output, diagnostic analytics could uncover factors impacting quality, predictive analytics might forecast maintenance needs, and prescriptive analytics could optimize production schedules. In healthcare, descriptive analytics might summarize patient data, diagnostic analytics could identify disease risk factors, predictive analytics might forecast patient outcomes, and prescriptive analytics could guide treatment plans. These analytics types across finance, marketing, energy, and beyond create a versatile toolkit for extracting insights and making impactful decisions.

While these analytics types offer immense potential, challenges related to data quality, bias, and ethical considerations require careful attention. Poor-quality data can lead to inaccurate insights and decisions. Bias in historical data might result in biased predictions. Ethical considerations arise in prescriptive analytics, where recommendations could have ethical implications. Interpretation of analytics results requires context and domain expertise to avoid misinformed decisions.

Descriptive, diagnostic, predictive, and prescriptive analytics form a multidimensional spectrum that guides organizations through the layers of data insight. Descriptive analytics lays the foundation by summarizing historical data, diagnostic analytics unravels causal relationships, predictive analytics anticipates future outcomes, and prescriptive analytics guides optimal decision-making. Integrating these analytics types empowers organizations to extract insights, make informed decisions, and optimize strategies. In an era defined by data, these analytics types stand as beacons, illuminating the path to knowledge, progress, and innovation across industries and domains. As organizations navigate the complexities of the digital age, the seamless integration of these analytics types fosters a comprehensive approach to decision-making, unlocking the power of data-driven excellence.

## Machine learning algorithms for big data analysis

In the era of big data, where massive volumes of information are generated at an unprecedented pace, traditional data analysis methods prove inadequate to extract meaningful insights from these complex datasets. Machine learning algorithms, designed to handle the intricacies of large-scale data, emerge as powerful tools for uncovering patterns, making predictions, and guiding decision-making. This section delves into the realm of machine learning algorithms for big data analysis, exploring various categories of algorithms such as classification, regression, clustering, and recommendation systems. By navigating through the intelligence landscape in vast datasets, we uncover how these algorithms empower organizations to extract actionable insights, enhance personalization, and drive transformative progress across diverse industries and domains.

Classification algorithms form the bedrock of supervised learning, where data is labeled to predict categorical outcomes. Algorithms like decision trees, random forests, support vector machines, and k-nearest neighbors enable data classification into predefined classes. In healthcare, these algorithms aid in diagnosing diseases based on patient symptoms and medical test results. In finance, they detect fraudulent transactions by categorizing them as genuine or fraudulent. The application of classification algorithms spans customer segmentation, sentiment analysis, image recognition, and more, making them essential tools for predictive modeling in diverse scenarios.

Regression algorithms focus on predicting continuous numerical values based on historical data patterns. Linear, polynomial, and support vector regression are examples of algorithms used to model relationships between variables and forecast outcomes. In real estate, regression algorithms predict property prices based on features like location, size, and amenities. In economics, they forecast economic indicators like GDP growth. Regression algorithms analyze historical data, enable organizations to anticipate trends, optimize resources, and make informed decisions in scenarios where continuous value prediction is paramount.

Clustering algorithms operate within the realm of unsupervised learning, where data lacks predefined labels. These algorithms group similar data points into clusters based on their inherent similarities. K-means clustering, hierarchical clustering, and DBSCAN are popular techniques in this category. Clustering algorithms find applications in diverse domains such as customer segmentation, image segmentation, and gene expression analysis. In retail, they aid in understanding purchasing patterns by grouping similar customer behaviors. In social networks, they reveal community structures and influencer dynamics. Clustering algorithms identify hidden patterns and facilitate data-driven decision-making when labeled data is scarce.

Recommendation systems, or collaborative filtering, focus on personalizing user experiences by suggesting relevant items or content. These algorithms analyze user preferences and historical behavior to make personalized recommendations. Content-based recommendation systems analyze item attributes to match user preferences, while collaborative filtering suggests items based on similar users' preferences. Recommendation systems find applications in e-commerce, streaming platforms, and social media. They enhance user engagement, increase sales, and optimize content delivery by tailoring experiences to individual preferences.

Ensemble methods harness the power of multiple machine learning algorithms to improve predictive accuracy and reduce overfitting. Techniques like bagging, boosting, and stacking combine the predictions of several base models to generate a stronger overall prediction. Random forests, a form of ensemble learning, aggregate predictions from multiple decision trees to enhance classification accuracy. Ensemble methods excel in scenarios where a single algorithm might struggle due to noisy or complex data. By combining algorithm strengths, ensemble methods provide robust solutions for big data analysis challenges.

Deep learning, a subset of machine learning, entails neural networks that simulate the structure of the human brain. Convolutional neural networks (CNNs) excel in image and video analysis, while recurrent neural networks (RNNs) handle sequential data like text and speech. Deep learning has transformed fields like computer vision, natural language processing, and speech recognition. In autonomous vehicles, CNNs detect pedestrians and road signs. In healthcare, RNNs analyze electronic health records for disease prediction. The depth and complexity of neural networks enable them to unearth intricate patterns within big data, making them indispensable tools in modern analytics.

While machine learning algorithms offer immense potential for big data analysis, they have challenges that warrant attention. Data quality and preprocessing are critical for accurate insights. Overfitting, where models perform well on training data but poorly on new data, requires regularization techniques. Bias in data can lead to biased predictions, and the "black box" nature of some algorithms raises concerns about interpretability and transparency. Ethical considerations emerge when algorithms make decisions that impact human lives. A deep understanding of algorithm behavior, domain expertise, and ethical guidelines is essential for responsible application.

Machine learning algorithms stand as beacons of intelligence in the vast landscape of big data analysis. From classification to regression, clustering to recommendation systems, these algorithms empower organizations to extract insights, predict trends, and enhance decision-making across diverse industries and domains. By harnessing the power of data-driven models, organizations unlock the potential of data to transform their strategies, optimize operations, and drive innovation. As the digital universe continues to expand, machine learning algorithms will remain instrumental in unraveling the complexities of data, illuminating the path to insights, knowledge, and data-driven excellence.

## Case studies illustrating successful analytics implementations

In the contemporary landscape, data has evolved into a strategic asset that organizations harness to drive informed decision-making, optimize operations, and innovate across diverse domains. Successful analytics implementations are beacons of this transformative power, showcasing how data-driven insights can shape strategies, enhance customer experiences, and revolutionize industries. This section delves into case studies that illustrate the triumphant implementation of analytics solutions, exploring instances where organizations have leveraged data to achieve remarkable outcomes. By examining these real-world examples, we uncover how analytics implementations have propelled organizations toward success, demonstrating the tangible impact of data-driven transformation.

*Case Study 1: Netflix's Personalization Revolution* The

powerhouse of streaming services, Netflix, is now synonymous with data-driven personalization, completely changing the way people watch content. By meticulously analyzing user viewing habits, preferences, and engagement metrics, Netflix employs collaborative filtering algorithms to provide personalized content recommendations. This analytics implementation has not only boosted customer engagement but has also transformed the entire media landscape. The success of Netflix's recommendation system serves as a testament to the power of analytics in revolutionizing content delivery, retaining subscribers, and shaping the future of entertainment consumption.

*Case Study 2: Walmart's Supply Chain Optimization* A

retail behemoth, Walmart harnesses analytics to optimize its supply chain, a critical component of its operations. Through applying predictive analytics and machine learning algorithms, Walmart analyzes factors like customer demand, inventory levels, and shipping routes to streamline its supply chain. By accurately forecasting demand and aligning inventory accordingly, Walmart minimizes stockouts, reduces excess inventory, and enhances overall operational efficiency. This analytics implementation has enabled Walmart to deliver products more effectively, reduce costs, and create a seamless customer shopping experience.

***Case Study 3: Airbnb's Dynamic Pricing Strategy*** Airbnb, a

disruptor in the hospitality industry, employs analytics to drive its dynamic pricing strategy. By analyzing factors like demand, location, and property attributes, Airbnb uses machine learning algorithms to adjust prices for accommodations dynamically. This analytics-driven approach optimizes revenue for hosts while providing competitive prices for guests. The success of Airbnb's dynamic pricing strategy demonstrates how analytics can transform traditional industries, empower individual hosts, and provide personalized experiences for travelers.

***Case Study 4: Predictive Maintenance at General Electric***

General Electric (GE), a multinational conglomerate, utilizes predictive analytics to revolutionize maintenance practices in the manufacturing sector. By analyzing sensor data from industrial equipment, GE's analytics solutions predict potential equipment failures before they occur. This implementation has transformed maintenance from reactive to proactive, minimizing downtime, reducing costs, and optimizing operations. GE's success in predictive maintenance highlights the potential of analytics to transform industrial practices, enhance productivity, and drive innovation in manufacturing.

*Case Study 5: Healthcare Transformation at Mount Sinai*

Mount Sinai Health System, a leading healthcare institution, leverages analytics to enhance patient care and outcomes. Through analyzing electronic health records, patient data, and medical research, Mount Sinai employs machine learning algorithms to predict disease risks, identify treatment options, and personalize patient interventions. This analytics implementation has led to improved patient outcomes, reduced hospital readmissions, and enhanced medical research capabilities. Mount Sinai's data-driven approach underscores the potential of analytics to revolutionize healthcare practices, improve patient well-being, and advance medical research.

*Case Study 6: Predictive Analytics in Financial Services at Capital One*

Capital One, a financial services company, harnesses analytics to transform its credit card business. Capital One employs predictive analytics to assess credit risk and tailor credit limits by analyzing customer spending patterns, credit histories, and financial behaviors. This analytics-driven approach enhances customer experiences by offering personalized financial solutions while minimizing credit risk for the company. Capital One's success in predictive analytics exemplifies how analytics can optimize financial services, mitigate risks, and provide value to both customers and organizations.

These case studies offer helpful insights into the potential of analytics implementations to drive transformative outcomes across industries. Lessons learned highlight the importance of data quality, domain expertise, and ethical considerations in analytics projects. Successful implementations require collaboration between data professionals, domain experts, and stakeholders to align analytics solutions with organizational objectives. As the digital era evolves, the impact of analytics implementations will grow, reshaping industries, enhancing customer experiences, and guiding organizations toward data-driven excellence.

While these case studies exemplify the triumphs of analytics implementations, challenges such as data privacy, bias, and ethical considerations must be addressed. Ensuring data's responsible and ethical use is paramount, especially when analytics solutions impact human lives and decisions. Protecting user privacy, mitigating bias, and maintaining transparency in algorithms are critical considerations for organizations embarking on analytics implementations.

The case studies presented illuminate the transformative potential of successful analytics implementations. From entertainment to retail, manufacturing to healthcare, these examples underscore how data-driven insights can revolutionize strategies, operations, and customer experiences. The success stories of Netflix, Walmart, Airbnb, General Electric, Mount Sinai, and Capital One exemplify the tangible impact of analytics on diverse industries, guiding organizations toward innovation and excellence. As the digital universe expands, analytics implementations stand as beacons of data-driven transformation, shaping a future driven by insights, knowledge, and the power of data-driven decision-making.

# CHAPTER VII

# Tools for Big Data Analysis

## Overview of popular big data analysis tools: Hadoop, Spark, etc.

In the digital age, the proliferation of data has led to the emergence of complex and diverse datasets, commonly called big data. As organizations seek to derive meaningful insights from these vast information repositories, powerful tools have arisen to address the challenges posed by data volume, variety, and velocity. Among these tools, Hadoop and Spark are pillars of big data analysis, offering distinct capabilities to process, manage, and analyze data at scale. This section overviews these popular big data analysis tools, highlighting their features, strengths, and applications in navigating the ever-evolving data processing landscape.

Hadoop, an open-source framework, revolutionized the field of big data analysis with its distributed computing capabilities. At its core, Hadoop comprises two key components: the MapReduce programming model and the HDFS (Hadoop Distributed File System). HDFS divides data into blocks and distributes them across multiple nodes, enabling efficient storage and retrieval of large datasets. MapReduce facilitates parallel data processing, allowing users to write programs that analyze data distributedly. This framework empowers organizations to tackle data-intensive tasks like batch processing, log analysis, and large-scale data transformations.

Hadoop's versatility extends to a variety of use cases across industries. Hadoop can analyze customer purchase histories in retail to identify shopping patterns and preferences. In finance, it can process large volumes of financial data to detect fraudulent transactions. In genomics, it can analyze DNA sequences to uncover insights into genetic traits. Hadoop's ability to handle massive datasets and its cost-effective open-source nature make it a staple tool in organizations seeking to harness the power of big data.

While Hadoop paved the way for big data processing, Apache Spark emerged as a complementary tool that significantly accelerates data analytics. Spark, another open-source framework, offers in-memory data processing capabilities, reducing the need for frequent data reads from disk. This enhancement results in faster processing speeds, making Spark ideal for iterative algorithms and interactive data analysis. Spark provides high-level APIs in languages like Java, Scala, Python, and R, simplifying the development of complex analytics applications.

Spark's versatility and performance have led to its adoption in various use cases. In machine learning, Spark's machine learning library, MLlib, enables organizations to train complex models on large datasets efficiently. In real-time analytics, Spark Streaming processes and analyzes data streams in real-time, facilitating applications like fraud detection and social media sentiment analysis. Spark GraphX specializes in graph processing, making it suitable for network analysis and social network applications.

Hadoop and Spark offer distinct strengths and trade-offs catering to different use cases. Hadoop excels in batch processing scenarios where data is read, processed, and written back to disk. It shines in scenarios with high data volumes that don't require real-time processing. However, Spark is well-suited for iterative and interactive data analysis due to its in-memory capabilities. It excels in scenarios that demand low-latency processing and interactive querying.

While Hadoop's MapReduce paradigm requires developers to write explicit code for each data processing step, Spark's high-level APIs simplify the development process. Spark's caching of data in memory reduces the need for repetitive data reads, resulting in improved processing speeds compared to Hadoop's disk-based processing.

In big data analysis, Hadoop and Spark stand as cornerstones, offering organizations the tools to navigate the complexities of data processing at scale. Hadoop's distributed file system and MapReduce model provide a foundation for efficient storage and batch processing. Spark's in-memory processing capabilities and high-level APIs accelerate data analysis and enable real-time processing. The selection between these tools depends on the specific use case, data processing requirements, and performance considerations.

As the landscape of big data evolves, Hadoop and Spark remain at the forefront, adapting to new challenges and technologies. Organizations that seek to harness the power of big data analysis can leverage these tools to uncover insights, drive innovation, and make informed decisions that shape the future of their industries. Whether processing petabytes of data or enabling real-time analytics, Hadoop and Spark empower data professionals to navigate the data-driven era confidently and efficiently.

# Cloud-based solutions for big data processing

In the digital age, the proliferation of data has given rise to the need for efficient and scalable processing solutions to extract valuable insights from large and complex datasets. Cloud computing has appeared as a transformative force, allowing organizations to process big data in a flexible, cost-effective, and scalable manner. This section explores the world of cloud-based solutions for big data processing, examining the advantages, challenges, and real-world applications of leveraging cloud platforms to unlock the potential of data-driven decision-making.

Cloud-based solutions present several advantages for big data processing that traditional on-premises approaches struggle to match. Scalability is a defining feature of cloud computing, enabling organizations to adjust processing resources as data volumes fluctuate seamlessly. This elasticity is particularly valuable for processing dynamic workloads, where spikes in data processing demands are common. Instead of investing in and managing on-premises hardware, organizations can provision resources on-demand, optimizing costs while ensuring high performance during peak times.

Flexibility is another hallmark of cloud-based solutions. The ability to choose from various data processing frameworks and tools allows organizations to tailor their solutions to specific use cases. Whether using Hadoop, Spark, or specialized cloud-native services, cloud platforms provide a rich ecosystem of tools designed to handle diverse data processing challenges. Moreover, the pay-as-you-go pricing model eliminates the need for upfront capital investments, making cloud-based solutions accessible to organizations of all sizes.

While cloud-based solutions offer compelling benefits, they come with challenges that require careful consideration. Data security and privacy concerns are paramount, especially when involving sensitive or regulated data. Organizations must ensure that cloud providers adhere to stringent security measures, data encryption protocols, and compliance standards to mitigate risks. Additionally, the potential for vendor lock- in should be addressed, as migrating from one cloud provider to another can be complex and costly.

Latency can also be a challenge, mainly when processing real-time data. While cloud platforms offer impressive scalability, data processing might involve data transfers between on-premises environments and the cloud, leading to latency issues that impact real-time analytics. Careful architectural design and data placement strategies can help mitigate latency concerns, but they require thorough planning and optimization.

Cloud-based solutions for big data processing find applications across industries, shaping how organizations operate, innovate, and interact with their data. In healthcare, cloud platforms enable the analysis of massive medical datasets to predict disease outbreaks, personalize treatments, and enhance patient care. In retail, real-time analytics on cloud platforms allow businesses to respond swiftly to changing market trends and customer preferences, optimizing inventory management and sales strategies.

Cloud-based big data processing is also revolutionizing finance, where scalable and flexible cloud solutions power data-intensive tasks like fraud detection, risk assessment, and algorithmic trading. In manufacturing, cloud platforms analyze sensor data from IoT devices to optimize production processes, minimize downtime, and enhance overall efficiency. Across these domains and more, cloud-based solutions are redefining how organizations process and leverage their data, enabling data-driven innovation and strategic decision-making.

Cloud-based solutions for big data processing stand as a transformative force in the data-driven landscape. The advantages of scalability, flexibility, and cost-effectiveness empower organizations to unlock the potential of their data, regardless of size or industry. As organizations embrace the era of data-driven excellence, cloud platforms provide the infrastructure and tools to process, analyze, and derive insights from vast and complex datasets. While security, privacy, and latency challenges persist, the benefits of cloud-based big data processing far outweigh the concerns. By harnessing the potential of cloud computing, organizations are positioned to thrive in an era defined by data, innovation, and the endless possibilities of data-driven decision-making.

## Choosing the right tools based on project requirements

In the fast-evolving landscape of data analysis and processing, the choice of tools plays a pivotal role in identifying the success of a project. Many tools and technologies are available, from big data analytics to machine learning, each offering distinct features and capabilities. However, the challenge lies in selecting the right tools that align with project requirements, goals, and constraints. This section delves into the intricacies of choosing the right tools based on project requirements, exploring the factors influencing selection, the importance of matching tools to specific tasks, and real-world considerations guiding technology decisions.

Choosing the right tools begins with thoroughly understanding the project's unique characteristics and objectives. Scalability is a fundamental consideration, as projects dealing with large datasets demand tools capable of effectively handling data volume and velocity. Compatibility with the existing technology stack is crucial, ensuring smooth integration with existing systems and workflows. Skill sets of the project team also influence tool selection, as familiarity and expertise with a particular tool can expedite project development and execution.

Budget constraints are another determining factor. While often cost-effective, open-source tools might lack certain features compared to commercial alternatives. The project's timeline also plays a role, as some tools are better suited for rapid development and prototyping, while others provide robust solutions for long-term projects. Flexibility to adapt to changing requirements is essential, considering the evolving nature of projects and technology.

Different project stages often require specialized tools to address specific tasks effectively. Tools like Pandas, NumPy, and OpenRefine provide data manipulation capabilities for data preprocessing and cleaning. When dealing with big data, Hadoop and Spark excel in distributed processing and analysis. For machine learning tasks, scikit-learn, TensorFlow, and PyTorch offer libraries to build and train models. Data visualization tools like Tableau and Power BI aid in presenting insights to stakeholders effectively.

The selection of tools should also consider the nature of data. Structured data might require relational databases, while unstructured data might demand NoSQL databases or text mining tools. The objectives of the analysis, whether descriptive, diagnostic, predictive, or prescriptive, also dictate the choice of tools and algorithms.

In practice, tool selection often involves navigating trade-offs. Choosing the most advanced tool might lead to complexity and steep learning curves for the team, potentially slowing down progress. On the other hand, opting for familiar tools might limit capabilities and miss out on innovations that newer tools offer. Balance is essential, ensuring that the chosen tools align with project goals while maximizing the efficiency and productivity of the team.

Vendor lock-in is another consideration, especially when choosing proprietary tools or cloud-based solutions. Lock-in might hinder future scalability and flexibility if switching tools become necessary. Evaluating the support and community around a tool is crucial, as vibrant communities offer resources, forums, and updates contributing to successful project implementation.

Tool selection is rarely a one-time decision but rather an iterative process that evolves as the project progresses. As project requirements evolve and new challenges arise, the initial tool choices might need to be reevaluated or supplemented with additional tools. Regular assessments and adaptations ensure that the chosen tools align with project goals and evolving needs.

Choosing the right tools based on project requirements is an art that combines understanding the unique project context, evaluating available options, and aligning tools with specific tasks. The array of tools available, from programming languages and frameworks to libraries and platforms, offers a rich toolkit to cater to diverse project needs. Organizations can make informed decisions that drive project success by carefully considering factors like scalability, compatibility, budget, and expertise. While trade-offs and considerations abound, the iterative nature of tool selection ensures that projects can adapt and thrive in the dynamic landscape of technology, ultimately achieving data-driven objectives and unlocking transformative results.

## Setting up and configuring big data analysis environments

The journey from raw data to meaningful insights requires a robust and well-configured environment in data analysis. As data complexity and volume continue to grow, setting up and configuring big data analysis environments becomes a critical step in the data processing pipeline. This section delves into the intricacies of creating optimal environments for big data analysis, exploring the components, considerations, and best practices that form the foundation for successful data-driven insights.

A well-structured big data analysis environment comprises several key components collaborating to process, analyze, and derive insights from vast datasets. Data storage is foundational, encompassing databases, data lakes, or data warehouses that house the raw and processed data. The choice of storage technology depends on factors like data structure, volume, and query complexity.

Data processing frameworks like Hadoop and Spark enable distributed processing across clusters of machines, addressing the challenges posed by large-scale data. These frameworks break down data processing tasks into smaller, parallelizable units, enhancing efficiency and scalability. Furthermore, data preprocessing and cleaning tools prepare raw data for analysis by handling missing values, outliers, and inconsistencies.

Data visualization tools are crucial in transforming raw insights into actionable information. Tools like Tableau, Power BI, and Matplotlib create visual representations of data trends, patterns, and relationships. These visualizations enhance data communication, enabling stakeholders to grasp insights more effectively.

Configuring a big data analysis environment involves a series of considerations that ensure optimal performance, security, and usability. Scalability is paramount, as environments must accommodate growing data volumes and processing demands. Scalable solutions might involve distributed storage systems, cluster management tools, and load balancing mechanisms to ensure efficient resource utilization.

Security is another critical consideration. Access controls, encryption, and authentication mechanisms safeguard sensitive data from unauthorized access. Regular updates and patches mitigate vulnerabilities that malicious actors might exploit.

Usability and accessibility are essential to facilitate efficient analysis workflows. User-friendly interfaces and intuitive tools enable data professionals to interact with the environment seamlessly. Ensuring that tools integrate smoothly with existing systems and technologies enhances efficiency and reduces friction in the analysis process.

Several best practices guide the setup and configuration of big data analysis environments. Starting with clear project objectives and requirements is fundamental, as they shape the components, tools, and technologies selection. It's crucial to align the environment with the project's goals to avoid overengineering or underdelivering.

Infrastructure as code (IaC) practices streamline environment setup and maintenance. Tools like Terraform and Ansible allow automated provisioning of resources, reducing manual errors and ensuring consistency across environments.

Monitoring and performance optimization are continuous activities. Implementing monitoring tools provides insights into resource utilization, bottlenecks, and potential issues. Regular performance tuning, resource allocation adjustments, and workload optimization ensure the environment operates efficiently.

The significance of setting up and configuring big data analysis environments becomes evident through real-world applications across industries. In e-commerce, an efficiently configured environment enables real-time customer behavior analysis, allowing businesses to make informed decisions on pricing, inventory management, and personalized recommendations.

In healthcare, well-structured environments process electronic health records, patient data, and medical research to predict disease outbreaks, personalize treatments, and enhance patient care. In finance, optimized environments power real-time analytics for fraud detection, risk assessment, and algorithmic trading, enabling rapid responses to market trends and security threats.

Setting up and configuring big data analysis environments is the bedrock upon which data-driven insights are built.

A carefully orchestrated combination of storage, processing, preprocessing, visualization, and security components forms a dynamic ecosystem that transforms raw data into actionable insights. By adhering to best practices and aligning configurations with project goals, organizations can create environments that empower data professionals to unravel patterns, uncover trends, and make knowledgeable decisions that drive innovation and success. As data continues to shape industries and drive transformative change, a well-configured big data analysis environment stands as the gateway to harnessing the power of data for strategic advantage.

# CHAPTER VIII

# Scalability and Performance Optimization

## Challenges of processing and analyzing massive datasets

In today's data-driven landscape, the information explosion has led to massive datasets offering unprecedented insights and innovation opportunities. However, with the vast potential of these datasets comes a unique set of challenges that organizations must navigate to extract meaningful value. Processing and analyzing massive datasets require addressing issues related to data volume, velocity, variety, quality, and computational complexity. This section delves into the complexities of dealing with massive datasets, exploring the challenges posed by their sheer size and intricacy, and discussing strategies to overcome these hurdles while unlocking the potential of data-driven decision-making.

Massive datasets, often measured in terabytes or petabytes, challenge traditional computing and storage infrastructures. As the volume of data increases, organizations face challenges in efficiently storing, managing, and accessing the data. Traditional relational databases might struggle with the scale, leading to slow query performance and increased latency. Scalable storage solutions like distributed file systems and cloud-based storage services address these challenges by enabling organizations to distribute data across multiple nodes and seamlessly scale resources as needed.

The term "data velocity" originated from the pace at which data is created and must be handled. In scenarios like social media, IoT devices, and financial transactions, data is generated in real-time, necessitating the ability to analyze and respond to the data promptly. Traditional batch processing approaches might be inadequate for real-time analytics. Solutions like stream processing frameworks and complex event processing tools enable organizations to process data as it arrives, allowing for immediate insights and responses to changing data patterns.

Massive datasets are often heterogeneous, comprising various data types such as structured, semi-structured, and unstructured data. Traditional relational databases are optimized for structured data but struggle with unstructured or semi-structured data like text, images, and sensor data. Organizations must grapple with the challenge of integrating and analyzing diverse data types to derive comprehensive insights. NoSQL databases, search engines, and specialized data processing frameworks provide solutions for handling and analyzing data with varying structures and formats.

Data quality is a critical challenge in the realm of massive datasets. As the volume of data grows, so does the likelihood of errors, inconsistencies, and noise. Ensuring accurate and reliable insights require data preprocessing and cleaning techniques to handle missing values, outliers, and discrepancies. Quality assurance processes, data validation rules, and automated data cleansing tools are crucial in maintaining data integrity and improving the accuracy of analysis outcomes.

The computational complexity of processing massive datasets requires careful resource allocation and performance optimization. Analyzing large datasets might demand significant computational power and memory resources, leading to challenges in hardware provisioning, parallel processing, and optimizing query performance. Distributed processing frameworks like Hadoop and Spark provide solutions for parallel execution of tasks across clusters of machines, while cloud-based services offer scalable resources to handle computational demands effectively.

The challenges of processing and analyzing massive datasets are multifaceted, requiring organizations to address issues related to data volume, velocity, variety, quality, and computational complexity. Navigating these challenges demands a combination of technological solutions, data management strategies, and domain expertise. Organizations can mitigate these challenges by leveraging scalable storage solutions, stream processing frameworks, specialized databases, and advanced data preprocessing techniques and unlock the potential of data-driven insights. Organizations aiming to prosper in the data-driven economy must grasp the intricacies of massive datasets in a world where data is growing exponentially. By embracing these challenges and applying innovative solutions, organizations can turn the complexity of data at scale into a source of strategic advantage, driving innovation, optimization, and informed decision-making.

## Techniques for scalability: parallel processing, distributed computing, etc.

In the era of big data and complex computational tasks, the ability to scale computing resources to match growing demands is essential for organizations aiming to process and analyze massive datasets efficiently. Scalability, the capacity to handle larger workloads seamlessly, hinges on the strategic use of techniques like parallel processing and distributed computing. This section delves into these techniques, exploring how they contribute to scalability, the challenges they address, and their role in enabling organizations to harness the full potential of their data- driven endeavors.

Parallel processing involves breaking down complex tasks into smaller, manageable units that can be executed simultaneously on multiple processing units, such as CPU cores or computing clusters. By distributing workloads across available resources, parallel processing significantly reduces the time required to complete computationally intensive tasks. This technique shines in scenarios like data analysis, image rendering, and simulations, where tasks can be divided into independent subtasks that do not rely on each other's results.

Parallel processing strategies vary, encompassing data parallelism and task parallelism. In data parallelism, identical operations are performed concurrently on different subsets of data. Task parallelism involves executing different tasks on separate processing units, often requiring synchronization mechanisms to manage dependencies between tasks.

Distributed computing takes scalability to another level by utilizing multiple interconnected machines, or nodes, to collectively process data and perform tasks. This approach extends beyond the capabilities of a single machine by aggregating computing power from multiple sources. Distributed computing frameworks like Hadoop and Spark exemplify this concept, enabling the processing of massive datasets that would overwhelm individual machines.

Distributed computing relies on effective data partitioning, task scheduling, and data communication mechanisms. Data is divided into smaller chunks, which are distributed across nodes for parallel processing. Tasks are intelligently scheduled to optimize resource utilization and minimize bottlenecks. Communication mechanisms enable nodes to exchange data and intermediate results, facilitating collaborative computation.

Parallel processing and distributed computing offer several advantages that enhance scalability and efficiency. Reduced execution time and improved performance are chief among these benefits. By leveraging multiple processing units, tasks are completed more swiftly, enabling organizations to analyze data and derive insights faster. Additionally, both techniques enhance fault tolerance, as the failure of a single node or processing unit does not result in complete task failure.

However, challenges persist. Coordinating tasks and data across distributed nodes requires careful management to ensure data consistency and task synchronization. Communication overhead and data transfer times might introduce latency that impacts overall performance. Moreover, designing algorithms and applications that effectively leverage parallelism and distribution requires a deep understanding of the problem domain and the underlying computing architecture.

Parallel processing and distributed computing find applications across industries, powering data analysis, simulations, scientific research, and more. In finance, parallel processing accelerates complex financial modeling and risk analysis. In genomics, distributed computing aids in the analysis of DNA sequences, enabling researchers to identify genetic traits and mutations. In weather forecasting, both techniques contribute to processing vast amounts of meteorological data, delivering timely and accurate predictions.

As data grows exponentially, the importance of scalability techniques becomes even more pronounced. Emerging technologies like edge computing and serverless computing further reshape scalability paradigms. Edge computing pushes computational power closer to data sources, reducing data transfer times and enhancing real-time processing capabilities. Serverless computing abstracts infrastructure management, allowing developers to focus solely on code, while cloud providers handle resource provisioning and scaling.

Scalability through parallel processing and distributed computing is at the heart of data-driven innovation. These techniques empower organizations to handle larger workloads, process massive datasets, and tackle complex tasks efficiently and quickly. By embracing parallelism and distribution, organizations can unlock the full potential of their computing resources, enabling insights, discoveries, and decisions that drive innovation and competitiveness. As technology evolves, scalability techniques remain indispensable tools in the data-driven era, propelling organizations toward a future where computational challenges are met with ingenuity and computational power.

# Performance optimization strategies

In data analysis, the pursuit of meaningful insights is often accompanied by the challenge of efficiently managing and processing large volumes of data. Performance optimization strategies are pivotal in maximizing the efficiency and speed of data analysis tasks, enabling organizations to extract valuable insights, make informed decisions, and drive innovation. This section explores the intricacies of performance optimization, delving into the techniques, tools, and best practices organizations can employ to enhance the efficiency of data analysis processes.

Performance optimization involves the process of improving the speed, responsiveness, and efficiency of data analysis tasks. It encompasses a spectrum of techniques that address various aspects of the data analysis pipeline, including data preprocessing, transformation, computation, and visualization. The ultimate goal is to reduce processing time, increase throughput, and promptly obtain data-driven insights.

Effective performance optimization begins with data profiling and analysis. By understanding the characteristics of the data, such as volume, distribution, and structure, organizations can tailor optimization strategies to match the specific attributes of the dataset. Profiling tools help identify bottlenecks, resource constraints, and opportunities for improvement, providing insights that guide optimization efforts.

In relational databases, indexing plays a crucial role in enhancing query performance. Indexes accelerate data retrieval by creating efficient data structures that allow for rapid lookup of records. Additionally, optimizing data storage involves strategies like compression and partitioning, which reduce storage requirements and improve data access times. These techniques ensure that data retrieval is swift and efficient, especially in scenarios involving complex queries or large datasets.

Optimizing data queries is a critical aspect of performance improvement. Query optimization involves rewriting queries, restructuring joins, and utilizing appropriate indexes to ensure efficient data retrieval. Tools and techniques like query planners and optimizers analyze query execution plans, identifying opportunities for optimization and selecting the most efficient execution paths.

As discussed previously, parallel processing and distributed computing significantly enhance performance by leveraging multiple processing units or nodes to complete tasks simultaneously. These techniques reduce processing times for computationally intensive tasks, making them particularly valuable for analyzing large datasets and complex computations.

Effective memory management strategies help avoid memory-related performance bottlenecks. Techniques like memory pooling and garbage collection optimize memory usage and reduce the likelihood of memory leaks. Conversely, caching involves storing frequently accessed data in memory for rapid retrieval, minimizing the need for repetitive disk reads and improving response times.

Choosing optimized algorithms and utilizing specialized libraries can expedite data processing. Many programming languages offer libraries that provide optimized implementations of common data manipulation and analysis tasks. Utilizing these libraries reduces the need for reinventing the wheel and ensures that data operations are performed efficiently.

Real-time processing and streaming techniques cater to scenarios where data must be analyzed and acted upon as it arrives. Stream processing frameworks like Apache Kafka and Apache Flink enable organizations to process and analyze real-time data, facilitating immediate responses to data-driven events and patterns.

Several best practices guide organizations in their pursuit of performance optimization. Profiling and benchmarking help identify performance bottlenecks and measure improvements accurately. Regular monitoring and performance testing ensure that optimizations remain effective as data volumes and workloads evolve.

Balancing optimization efforts with maintainability is crucial. Over-optimization might lead to complex code that is hard to maintain and debug. Prioritizing optimization efforts based on critical tasks and data analysis pipelines ensures that resources are allocated where they have the most significant impact.

Performance optimization strategies lie at the heart of efficient data analysis, empowering organizations to process, analyze, and derive data insights quickly and precisely. Organizations can overcome data volume and computational complexity by employing techniques such as data profiling, indexing, query optimization, parallel processing, and memory management. As data continues to shape industries and drive decision-making, the application of performance optimization strategies becomes an essential element in harnessing the power of data for innovation, optimization, and strategic advantage.

## Monitoring and managing big data processing pipelines

In the dynamic landscape of big data analysis, the successful processing and analysis of vast datasets rely not only on sophisticated algorithms and powerful hardware but also on effective monitoring and management of data processing pipelines. Big data processing pipelines encompass a series of interconnected stages, from data ingestion and preprocessing to analysis and visualization. This section delves into the intricacies of monitoring and managing big data processing pipelines, exploring the significance of real-time tracking, challenges in ensuring pipeline reliability, and best practices that organizations can adopt to optimize data workflows and drive data-driven excellence.

Real-time monitoring is a cornerstone of effective big data processing pipeline management. It involves tracking data processing stages' health, performance, and progress as they unfold. Real-time monitoring empowers organizations to detect anomalies, bottlenecks, and errors early in the pipeline, allowing for immediate intervention and mitigation. Without robust monitoring, issues that arise might go unnoticed, leading to data inaccuracies, prolonged processing times, and compromised analysis outcomes.

Monitoring encompasses various aspects, including data quality checks, resource utilization, latency, throughput, and error rates. Real-time dashboards and visualizations provide stakeholders with insights into pipeline performance, enabling them to promptly make informed decisions and address issues. Monitoring tools and solutions offer alerts and notifications that trigger when predefined thresholds are exceeded, enabling swift responses to deviations from expected behavior.

Managing big data processing pipelines comes with its share of challenges. One significant challenge is ensuring pipeline reliability and fault tolerance. The sheer complexity of pipelines, with multiple interconnected stages and dependencies, increases the likelihood of failures. A single failure in a data processing stage can disrupt the entire pipeline, resulting in data loss, analysis delays, and compromised insights.

Another challenge lies in data consistency and integrity. Pipelines involving multiple data sources and transformations require mechanisms to ensure data remains consistent and accurate throughout the pipeline. Ensuring proper error handling, retry mechanisms, and data validation processes is vital to maintain the reliability of the pipeline.

Several best practices guide organizations in effectively monitoring and managing big data processing pipelines. Beginning with a comprehensive understanding of the pipeline's architecture, data sources, transformations, and destinations is crucial. Mapping out dependencies and potential failure points helps design robust monitoring strategies.

Adopting a data-driven approach to monitoring involves setting up automated data quality checks and validation processes at various stages of the pipeline. These checks ensure that data meets predefined quality standards and that errors are caught early in the process.

Implementing continuous integration and continuous deployment, or CI/CD practices streamlines the management of pipelines. Automated testing, version control, and deployment pipelines enable rapid iterations, reducing the likelihood of errors and improving pipeline stability.

The significance of monitoring and managing big data processing pipelines is exemplified through real-world applications across industries. In e-commerce, real-time monitoring ensures that customer transaction data is processed accurately, enabling timely inventory updates and sales analytics. In healthcare, monitoring pipeline stages ensures that patient data is securely processed and analyzed, contributing to personalized treatments and medical research.

Monitoring and managing big data processing pipelines form the backbone of efficient data analysis workflows. Real-time monitoring enables organizations to detect and address issues early, ensuring data accuracy, timely analysis, and informed decision-making. By adopting best practices that emphasize pipeline reliability, data integrity, and automation, organizations can optimize their data workflows and harness the power of big data to drive innovation, optimization, and strategic advantage. As data continues to shape industries and redefine business operations, effective pipeline monitoring and management remain essential elements in navigating the complex landscape of data-driven excellence.

# CHAPTER IX

# Data Visualization and Communication

## Importance of effective data visualization

In data analysis and decision-making, effective data visualization emerges as a powerful tool that transcends numbers and spreadsheets, transforming intricate datasets into understandable insights. Being able to communicate patterns, trends, and linkages becomes critical as data volume and complexity increase. This section delves into the significance of effective data visualization, exploring how visual representations enhance understanding, aid decision-making, and unlock the potential of data-driven insights across diverse industries and domains.

Data analysis often involves grappling with intricate datasets that harbor valuable insights within their complexities. Effective data visualization bridges raw data and actionable insights, distilling complex information into visual representations that are easily digestible and interpretable. Visualizations condense vast amounts of data into visual forms such as charts, graphs, heatmaps, and interactive dashboards. These visualizations enable data professionals and stakeholders to quickly grasp patterns, trends, and outliers, transcending raw data's complexity.

The human brain is inherently wired to process visual information efficiently. When presented with visuals, people absorb and retain information more effectively than when confronted with textual or numerical data alone. Effective data visualization thus enhances understanding by capitalizing on the brain's visual processing capabilities. It simplifies complex concepts, making them accessible to individuals with varying levels of data literacy. By offering a visual narrative, data visualizations facilitate effective communication among data professionals, analysts, and decision-makers, ensuring that insights are comprehensively conveyed and understood.

Data-driven decision-making hinges on the ability to extract meaningful insights from data. Effective data visualization is pivotal in this process by providing decision-makers with a clear, concise, and visual representation of relevant information. Visualizations highlight key trends, correlations, and anomalies, enabling stakeholders to make informed choices based on evidence rather than intuition. Whether it's identifying market trends, evaluating performance metrics, or optimizing resource allocation, data visualization empowers decision-makers to navigate complexity and derive actionable insights that drive positive outcomes.

Effective data visualization is about presenting existing insights, uncovering hidden patterns, and facilitating discoveries. Visualizations often reveal relationships and trends that are not apparent from raw data alone. Interactive visualizations enable users to explore data from different angles, enabling them to unearth unexpected insights and formulate new hypotheses. This iterative process of exploration and discovery is instrumental in driving innovation and advancing understanding in diverse fields, from scientific research to business analytics.

The importance of effective data visualization is exemplified by its applications across various industries. Visualizations help medical professionals analyze patient data, track disease outbreaks, and personalize treatments in healthcare. In finance, visualizing market trends and investment performance aids traders and analysts in making strategic decisions. In marketing, visualizations illustrate customer behavior and campaign effectiveness, guiding marketers in optimizing strategies. From education and environmental science to urban planning and social sciences, data visualization is a universal language that transcends disciplines and empowers data-driven decision-making.

Effective data visualization is a beacon of clarity amidst complexity in an era marked by data abundance. By translating intricate datasets into visual narratives, data visualization empowers individuals to understand, communicate, and act upon data-driven insights. Transforming intricate data into easily understood visualizations promotes creativity, quick decision-making, and a culture of data-driven excellence. As organizations and individuals harness the power of effective data visualization, they unlock the potential of data to transform industries, spark discoveries, and shape the future. In a world where data reigns supreme, the art and science of data visualization become an essential catalyst for realizing the full value of information and embracing the opportunities it brings.

## Choosing the right visualization techniques

In data analysis, the journey from raw data to actionable insights hinges on the art and science of visualization. Choosing the right visualization techniques is crucial to this process, as it determines how effectively data is transformed into understandable and meaningful narratives. With various visualization options available, selecting the appropriate technique requires a strategic approach considering data characteristics, objectives, and audience. This section delves into the significance of choosing the right visualization techniques, exploring the factors influencing these choices, and discussing best practices for creating visualizations that resonate, communicate, and inspire informed decision-making.

Effective visualization begins with a deep understanding of the data at hand and the objectives of the analysis. Different data types—such as categorical, numerical, temporal, and spatial—call for distinct visualization techniques that emphasize the data's inherent characteristics. For instance, bar charts and pie charts are well-suited for representing categorical data distributions, while scatter plots and line charts showcase trends and relationships in numerical data.

Similarly, the objectives of the analysis guide the choice of visualization techniques. Exploratory analyses may require interactive visualizations that allow users to manipulate and explore data subsets. For comparative analyses, side-by-side bar charts or box plots can effectively highlight differences between categories. On the other hand, storytelling visualizations may rely on narrative-driven techniques like infographics or flowcharts to guide audiences through complex concepts.

Selecting the right visualization technique involves matching the chosen method to the specific data and analytical tasks. For instance, geospatial data is best represented through maps, choropleth maps, or heatmaps, allowing patterns to emerge across geographical regions. On the other hand, time-series data can be effectively communicated through line charts, area charts, or stacked bar charts, depending on the insights sought.

Analytical tasks also influence technique selection. Identifying trends might call for line charts or scatter plots, while comparing proportions could involve bar charts or treemaps. Visualizing distributions may involve histograms, box plots, or density plots, providing a comprehensive view of data spread and central tendencies. Ultimately, the technique should serve the analytical goals by highlighting the most relevant information.

The audience and context play a pivotal role in technique selection. Different audiences have varying levels of data literacy and familiarity with visualization types. While a technical audience might appreciate complex visualizations like parallel coordinates or Sankey diagrams, a non-technical audience might resonate more with simpler bar charts or pie charts. Context, such as the platform on which the visualization will be presented—a research paper, presentation, or interactive dashboard— also influences technique choice.

Balancing familiarity and innovation is key. While innovative visualizations might captivate audiences, they must not sacrifice clarity or comprehension. Familiar visualizations resonate with audiences and facilitate quick understanding, but they must not compromise on accurately representing data insights.

Choosing the right visualization techniques is rarely a one-step process. Iterative design, where visualizations are refined based on feedback and testing, ensures that selected techniques effectively convey insights. Seeking feedback from colleagues, stakeholders, or potential users helps identify areas of improvement and guarantees that the visualization resonates with the intended audience. Based on user feedback, adjusting colors, scales, labels, and interactivity refines the visualization's impact and utility.

Choosing the right visualization techniques is an art that merges data understanding, analytical objectives, audience awareness, and design insight. As organizations harness the power of data to drive innovation and decision-making, the ability to strategically select visualizations that effectively convey insights becomes paramount. By aligning technique choices with data characteristics, objectives, audience preferences, and contextual factors, data professionals can craft visual narratives that transcend numbers and statistics, transforming data into insights that inspire action, drive understanding, and shape informed decisions in the data-driven era.

## Tools and libraries for creating impactful visualizations

In data analysis and communication, the power of impactful visualizations lies in the insights they convey and the tools and libraries that enable their creation. As the demand for clear, engaging, and informative data narratives grows, the availability of advanced tools and libraries becomes instrumental in crafting visualizations that resonate with audiences and drive decision-making.

This section explores the significance of tools and libraries for creating impactful visualizations, delving into the capabilities of popular platforms, discussing the role of programming languages and libraries, and highlighting best practices for harnessing technology to transform data into compelling visual stories.

Many platforms exist to facilitate visual exploration and creation, catering to individuals with varying levels of technical expertise. Widely used tools like Tableau, Power BI, and QlikView offer user-friendly interfaces that enable users to create interactive visualizations without in-depth coding knowledge. These platforms provide drag-and-drop functionality, pre-built templates, and seamless data integration, allowing data professionals to focus on design and insights rather than coding intricacies.

Open-source platforms like D3.js offer unparalleled flexibility and customization. D3.js, based on web technologies such as HTML, CSS, and SVG, empowers users to create intricate and interactive visualizations by manipulating data-driven documents. While D3.js requires programming skills, its flexibility allows for the creation of highly tailored visualizations that push the boundaries of functionality and design.

Programming languages are pivotal in creating impactful visualizations, offering data professionals a range of libraries and frameworks that streamline the process. Python, for instance, boasts libraries like Matplotlib, Seaborn, and Plotly that provide versatile tools for generating various visualizations. While Plotly focuses on interactive visualizations that may be integrated into presentations or web applications, Matplotlib and Seaborn provide a wide variety of chart types.

R, another popular programming language, features the ggplot2 package, celebrated for its ability to generate elegant and customizable visualizations. The package follows the grammar of graphics paradigm, enabling users to build complex visualizations through simple, structured syntax.

The ability to create impactful visualizations often hinges on interactivity and animation. Libraries like Plotly and Bokeh specialize in interactive visualizations that enable users to explore data, uncover insights, and manipulate variables. Interactivity is particularly valuable when conveying complex relationships or allowing users to drill down into specific data subsets.

Animation, too, plays a role in enhancing the impact of visualizations. Libraries like D3.js and Animate.css enable the creation of dynamic, attention-grabbing animations that guide audiences through data narratives. Animated transitions, bar chart race visualizations, and data-driven storytelling techniques captivate viewers and make data narratives more engaging.

While tools and libraries offer immense potential, their effective utilization relies on adhering to best practices. Firstly, understanding the data and the story it conveys is essential. Visualizations must accurately represent insights while avoiding misinterpretation or distortion. Choosing appropriate chart types that align with the data's characteristics and the narrative's objectives enhances clarity and comprehension.

Consistency in design, including color schemes, fonts, and layout, contributes to visualizations' overall aesthetic appeal and professionalism. Embracing simplicity and decluttering visuals ensures that the audience focuses on the data insights. Accessibility considerations, such as color choices for individuals with color blindness, ensure that visualizations are inclusive and can be understood by diverse audiences.

Tools and libraries for creating impactful visualizations form a symphony where creativity and technology harmoniously blend. With many platforms, programming languages, and libraries at their disposal, data professionals can transform data into compelling narratives that inform, inspire, and empower decision-making. By choosing the right tools based on expertise and requirements, data professionals unlock the potential to convey insights that transcend numbers, converting data into stories that captivate, engage, and drive action in the data-driven era.

## Communicating insights to non-technical stakeholders

In the data-driven landscape of today's organizations, the ability to glean actionable insights from complex datasets is a prized asset. Yet, the true value of these insights lies in their effective communication to non-technical stakeholders who may lack familiarity with data intricacies. Bridging the gap between data and understanding requires a skillful blend of visualization, storytelling, and empathy. This section explores the significance of communicating insights to non-technical stakeholders, delving into strategies that enhance clarity, facilitate engagement, and empower decision-making across diverse industries and domains.

Non-technical stakeholders, such as executives, managers, and clients, often lack the specialized knowledge of data analysis techniques and terminologies. Communicating complex insights to these stakeholders presents a unique challenge that demands data professionals to translate data-driven findings into relatable narratives. Overwhelming stakeholders with technical jargon and detailed methodologies can lead to confusion and hinder the actionable impact of insights.

Visualizations serve as powerful tools for translating complex data into easily digestible narratives. Choosing visualizations that align with the narrative and resonate with the audience is essential. Clear and concise visualizations, such as bar charts, line charts, and pie charts, provide straightforward representations of trends, comparisons, and proportions. Interactive elements in visualizations, like hover tooltips or filtering options, allow stakeholders to explore data at their own pace, enhancing engagement and understanding.

Infographics condense complex concepts into visually appealing snapshots with their combination of text and visuals. They distill intricate insights into easy-to-understand visuals, making them an effective medium for communicating high-level takeaways to non-technical audiences.

Storytelling is a potent vehicle for communicating insights, framing data within relatable contexts. A compelling data-driven story features a clear structure: a beginning that introduces the problem or context, a middle that explores data analysis and findings, and an end that presents actionable insights and implications. The narrative should guide stakeholders through the data exploration journey, fostering a deeper connection to the insights presented.

Incorporating real-world examples and relatable anecdotes humanizes the data, making it more accessible to non-technical stakeholders. Analogies that draw parallels between data trends and everyday experiences enhance understanding and engagement.

Understanding the audience's perspective and information needs is crucial. Empathy allows data professionals to anticipate questions and concerns, tailoring communication to address specific interests. Presenting insights that directly relate to the stakeholders' objectives and responsibilities resonates more effectively and establishes a meaningful connection between the data and its impact on the stakeholders' goals.

Engaging non-technical stakeholders involves inviting them to participate in the exploration of data insights. Interactive dashboards and presentations empower stakeholders to manipulate visualizations, ask questions, and gain deeper insights on their terms. This involvement fosters a sense of ownership and encourages stakeholders to derive insights directly, fostering a sense of ownership and enhancing the relevance of the insights to their decision-making.

Communication is a two-way street, and seeking feedback from non-technical stakeholders is crucial for refining communication strategies. Feedback sessions allow data professionals to understand where clarifications are needed and what resonates most with the audience. Adapting communication based on feedback ensures that insights are communicated effectively and contribute to meaningful actions and decisions.

Translating complex data insights to non-technical stakeholders is an art that demands both technical expertise and effective communication skills. By embracing visualizations, storytelling, empathy, and interactivity, data professionals bridge the gap between data complexities and understanding, empowering non-technical stakeholders to make informed decisions that drive innovation and growth. In a world where data-driven insights are pivotal, the ability to convey these insights with clarity, relevance, and impact is the linchpin that transforms data into actionable wisdom for the betterment of organizations and society.

# CHAPTER X

# Future Trends in Data Science and Big Data

## Emerging technologies and trends in the field

The domain of data science and big data is undergoing unparalleled development, propelled by technology breakthroughs that hold the potential to revolutionize industries, alter decision-making processes, and open up new opportunities for knowledge acquisition. As organizations grapple with increasingly vast and complex datasets, emerging technologies and trends emerge as guiding lights, illuminating the path toward more efficient analysis, enhanced insights, and greater value extraction. This section delves into the realm of emerging technologies and trends in data science and big data, exploring the potential of artificial intelligence (AI), machine learning (ML), edge computing, and ethical considerations, while highlighting the transformative power these innovations hold.

Artificial intelligence and machine learning stand as the cornerstones of data science's future, potentially revolutionizing how data is analyzed and utilized. AI is a wide range of technologies that simulate human cognitive functions, allowing computers to process information, learn from it, and adjust over time. Machine learning, a subset of AI, equips systems with the ability to learn patterns and make predictions from data without being explicitly programmed.

In the context of big data, AI and ML hold promise in automating data analysis processes, recognizing intricate patterns that humans might overlook, and predicting future trends with unprecedented accuracy. Techniques like deep learning, natural language processing (NLP), and reinforcement learning propel data science toward realms previously considered unattainable. Applications span industries —healthcare diagnosis, financial forecasting, recommendation systems, and even autonomous vehicles.

As the volume of data generated skyrockets, edge computing emerges as a game-changing paradigm in data analysis. By processing and analyzing data nearer to the source, edge computing eliminates the need to transfer massive volumes of data to centralized cloud servers. This decentralized approach mitigates latency issues, improves real-time decision-making, and enhances privacy by reducing the need to send sensitive data to external servers.

In the big data landscape, edge computing paves the way for real-time analytics in scenarios like Internet of Things (IoT) applications and smart cities. Sensor data can be processed locally to trigger immediate responses, from adjusting traffic signals to detecting anomalies in manufacturing processes. As edge computing continues to mature, its integration with data science enables organizations to extract insights closer to the data source, ushering in a new era of responsiveness and efficiency.

The proliferation of data also raises ethical considerations that demand careful attention. Data security, privacy, and responsible AI and ML technology use become critical. Safeguarding sensitive information and upholding legal and ethical standards in collecting and analyzing data are essential to preserving the trust of the public.

Emerging technologies like differential privacy and federated learning address privacy concerns by anonymizing and protecting individual data while enabling scale analysis. Transparency in AI decision-making, avoiding algorithmic biases, and fostering accountability in using data-driven insights become essential elements in the responsible deployment of emerging technologies.

The transformative power of emerging technologies and trends in data science and big data resonates across industries and domains. In healthcare, AI-driven diagnostics accelerate disease detection and treatment personalization. In finance, predictive analytics and algorithmic trading optimize investment decisions. Environmental monitoring leverages data science to predict natural disasters and manage resources sustainably.

Emerging technologies enable organizations to unearth insights from vast datasets that were previously untapped. The ability to process and analyze data at unprecedented scales fosters innovation and empowers decision-makers with foresight, allowing them to navigate complex landscapes with greater precision and strategic insight.

The transformative influence of emerging technologies and trends marks the trajectory of data science and big data. The convergence of AI, ML, edge computing, and ethical considerations reshapes the data analysis landscape, empowering organizations to glean insights, make informed decisions, and drive progress. As these technologies mature and intertwine, the potential for groundbreaking discoveries, enhanced efficiency, and ethical data utilization becomes increasingly tangible. Navigating the future of data science demands a keen understanding of these trends, a commitment to responsible practices, and a mindset that embraces innovation while prioritizing the well-being of individuals, society, and the ever-expanding realm of data.

## The role of AI as well as machine learning in shaping data analysis

In the dynamic landscape of data analysis, the convergence of artificial intelligence (AI) and machine learning (ML) stands as a transformative force reshaping how organizations derive insights from their vast datasets. AI and ML are not merely buzzwords; they represent a paradigm shift that empowers data professionals to unlock patterns, trends, and correlations that were previously hidden amidst data complexities. This section delves into the pivotal role of AI and machine learning in shaping data analysis, exploring how these technologies drive automation, enhance accuracy, and amplify the potential for discovery across diverse industries and domains.

At the core of AI and machine learning's impact on data analysis lies the ability to automate tasks that were previously manual and time-consuming. Traditional data analysis involved manual data cleaning, transformation, and feature engineering, consuming substantial resources and leaving room for human errors. AI and ML techniques, however, can automate these tasks with remarkable precision.

Automated data preprocessing tools can detect missing values, outliers, and inconsistencies, ensuring the data is clean and ready for analysis. Feature engineering, a critical step in extracting meaningful insights from data, can be automated through techniques that identify relevant features and create new ones, reducing the burden on data professionals and accelerating analysis pipelines.

AI and ML techniques augment data analysis by delivering a level of accuracy and predictive power that is unmatched by traditional approaches. Machine learning models can recognize intricate patterns, nonlinear relationships, and interactions within the data that might go unnoticed through manual analysis. These models learn from data and improve over time, adapting to changing patterns and evolving datasets.

In predictive analytics, AI-driven algorithms can forecast future trends, identify potential risks, and recommend optimal strategies. This capability empowers organizations to make informed decisions based on evidence rather than intuition, leading to improved outcomes across marketing, finance, and healthcare domains.

AI and machine learning enable advanced analytics by processing vast volumes of data and identifying complex relationships that drive more profound insights. Clustering algorithms can segment data into meaningful groups, revealing customer segments, market segments, or disease clusters. Association rule mining can uncover hidden relationships within transaction data, aiding in recommendation systems and market basket analysis.

In image and text analysis, AI and ML techniques excel in sentiment analysis, image recognition, and natural language processing tasks. These capabilities empower organizations to derive insights from unstructured data sources, providing a more holistic understanding of customer preferences, market sentiments, and emerging trends.

The role of AI as well as machine learning in data analysis transcends industry boundaries, finding applications in sectors ranging from healthcare and finance to manufacturing and entertainment. AI algorithms analyze medical images in healthcare to aid in diagnoses, while ML models predict patient outcomes and recommend personalized treatments. In finance, algorithms assess market trends, manage risk, and optimize investment portfolios. In manufacturing, AI-powered predictive maintenance minimizes downtime and increases efficiency.

In the entertainment sector, recommendation systems powered by AI and ML suggest movies, songs, and content based on individual preferences and behavior patterns. These systems enhance user experiences and drive engagement by delivering tailored recommendations that align with users' tastes.

The trajectory of AI and machine learning in shaping data analysis is marked by continuous advancement and innovation. As these technologies mature, challenges and ethical considerations come to the forefront. Algorithmic biases, data privacy concerns, and transparency in decision-making demand vigilant attention to ensure that AI and ML-driven insights are not only accurate but also fair and responsible.

The role of AI as well as machine learning in shaping data analysis transcends the confines of technology—it empowers organizations to navigate complexities, make data-driven decisions, and unravel insights that drive innovation and progress. Automation, enhanced accuracy, and advanced analytics become cornerstones guiding data professionals toward discovery. As AI and ML continue to evolve, their integration into data analysis processes holds the promise of a future where insights are more precise and accessible, democratizing the power of data-driven decision-making and propelling industries toward new horizons of excellence.

## Ethical and societal implications of big data usage

As the world becomes increasingly data-driven, using big data has become a double-edged sword, heralding immense opportunities and posing intricate ethical and societal challenges. The extensive amounts of data generated and collected offer the potential to transform industries, inform decision-making, and improve human lives. However, the power of big data comes with significant responsibilities, raising concerns about privacy, bias, consent, and the broader societal impact of data usage. This section delves into the ethical and societal implications of big data usage, exploring the delicate balance between innovation and responsibility, while examining the critical areas where thoughtful consideration and action are imperative.

One of the foremost ethical considerations in big data usage revolves around privacy and data protection. The sheer volume and granularity of data collected—from personal information to online behaviors—raise concerns about individual privacy. Organizations must navigate the intricate landscape of data anonymization, pseudonymization, and consent to ensure that data subjects' rights are respected. The potential for re-identification, where seemingly anonymized data can be linked back to individuals, underscores the need for robust safeguards and mechanisms that prevent unauthorized access or misuse.

Implementing regulations like the General Data Protection Regulation and the California Consumer

Privacy Act underscores the recognition of privacy as a fundamental right in the digital age. Organizations must grapple with compliance, transparency, and data minimization, balancing innovation and protecting individuals' personal information.

The algorithms and models underpinning big data analytics are not immune to biases present in the data they analyze. Biased data can lead to biased outcomes, perpetuating social inequities and systemic injustices. From recruitment algorithms favoring certain demographic groups to predictive policing systems disproportionately targeting marginalized communities, the impact of algorithmic bias reverberates across domains.

Ethical considerations dictate algorithm development's need for fairness, accountability, and transparency. Regular audits, ongoing monitoring, and diverse representation in data collection and model creation are essential to mitigate bias and ensure that the benefits of big data are equitably distributed.

The ethical principle of informed consent becomes particularly complex in the era of big data. The sheer volume of data collected—from online interactions to sensor data—renders traditional consent forms insufficient. Users may not fully comprehend the extent to which their data is collected, analyzed, and used for various purposes. The challenge lies in balancing enabling informed decision-making and ensuring that users are not overwhelmed by lengthy privacy policies.

Tools like transparent data dashboards and simplified consent mechanisms strive to enhance user autonomy, enabling individuals to understand and control the data they share. Organizations are tasked with adopting user-centric approaches that prioritize clarity, simplicity, and meaningful data sharing and usage choices.

The societal implications of big data extend beyond individual privacy concerns, touching on broader dynamics that shape societies. The accumulation of vast datasets enables organizations and governments to influence behavior, shape public opinion, and impact social narratives. The concentration of data and power in the hands of a few raises questions about democratic processes, individual agency, and the potential for manipulation.

The advent of surveillance capitalism, where personal data is commodified for profit, underscores the need for ethical considerations that safeguard individual rights and democratic values. The ethical use of big data necessitates transparency, accountability, and mechanisms that empower individuals to make informed choices about their data.

Big data usage's ethical and societal implications weave a complex tapestry that intertwines technological progress with human values. As organizations harness the potential of data-driven insights, they are responsible for navigating this intricate landscape with integrity, empathy, and a commitment to ethical principles.

Balancing innovation with respect for privacy, mitigating bias, ensuring informed consent, and addressing the broader societal impact of data usage require a collaborative effort from stakeholders across industries, governments, academia, and civil society. By embracing ethical considerations as an integral part of big data strategies, organizations pave the way for a future where data-driven advancements coexist harmoniously with individual rights, social justice, and the betterment of societies as a whole.

## Opportunities and challenges for future data scientists

The rapid evolution of technology and the exponential growth of data have ushered in an era of unprecedented opportunities and challenges for future data scientists. As organizations across industries recognize the value of data-driven insights, the demand for skilled professionals who can navigate complex datasets, unravel patterns, and extract meaningful insights has soared. This section delves into the multifaceted landscape that awaits future data scientists, exploring the diverse opportunities that lie ahead and the intricate challenges they must overcome to thrive in an ever-changing world of data-driven innovation.

The opportunities for future data scientists are as vast as the datasets they analyze. With the proliferation of IoT devices, social media platforms, and interconnected systems, data streams are becoming more diverse, dynamic, and voluminous. Future data scientists have the chance to harness these rich data sources to uncover insights that drive innovation across domains.

In healthcare, data scientists can contribute to personalized medicine by analyzing patient data to tailor treatment plans. In manufacturing, predictive maintenance fueled by data insights optimizes operations and minimizes downtime. In retail, recommendation algorithms enhance customer experiences and drive sales. The ability to turn data into actionable insights empowers data scientists to play a pivotal role in shaping the future of industries.

Future data scientists are not confined to silos of data analysis. The interdisciplinary nature of data science demands collaboration with domain experts, statisticians, software engineers, and business leaders. Data scientists must effectively communicate insights to non-technical stakeholders, bridging the gap between data complexities and business decisions.

The convergence of skills from diverse backgrounds creates a symbiotic relationship where data scientists learn domain-specific nuances, while domain experts gain the ability to leverage data-driven insights for informed decision-making. This collaboration amplifies the impact of data science, yielding solutions that resonate with real-world challenges and opportunities.

Ethical considerations become paramount as data scientists navigate a world driven by algorithms and predictions. The choices made in data collection, analysis, and model development carry far-reaching implications. Bias in algorithms, privacy concerns, and the responsible use of AI-generated insights demand vigilant attention.

Future data scientists are tasked with deriving insights and ensuring that these insights align with ethical standards. Transparency, fairness, and accountability must be woven into the fabric of data science practices. Responsible innovation requires data scientists to advocate for ethical decision-making, safeguarding individuals' rights while harnessing the potential of data-driven advancements.

The field of data science is marked by constant evolution. As technologies, tools, and techniques evolve, future data scientists must embrace a mindset of continuous learning. Staying updated with the latest advancements in machine learning, AI, big data frameworks, and programming languages is essential to stay relevant in an ever-changing landscape.

However, learning extends beyond technical skills. Developing communication, critical thinking, and problem-solving abilities enhance the efficacy of data scientists in conveying insights and tackling complex challenges. Adapting to new tools, paradigms, and problem domains fosters resilience in the face of uncertainty.

While opportunities abound, future data scientists must also grapple with challenges that come hand in hand with data-driven innovation. The explosion of data often leads to information overload, requiring data scientists to sift through noise to identify meaningful signals. The dynamic nature of data necessitates adapting analysis methods to evolving datasets.

Data security and privacy concerns loom large, particularly in the age of data breaches and cyber threats. Safeguarding sensitive information while extracting insights demands expertise in data encryption, access controls, and ethical data handling practices.

The realm of data science beckons future professionals to become pioneers of innovation, ethical stewardship, and informed decision-making. The opportunities for meaningful contributions span industries, from healthcare and finance to education and beyond. However, to realize these opportunities, future data scientists must navigate a landscape of complexity, interdisciplinary collaboration, ethical considerations, and continuous learning.

Embracing these challenges with diligence and enthusiasm equips data scientists with the tools to transform data into actionable insights that shape industries, drive progress, and enhance the human experience. As stewards of data-driven innovation, future data scientists stand on the precipice of a dynamic future, where the insights they uncover and the ethical standards they uphold will steer societies toward a more informed, equitable, and innovative future.

# CONCLUSION

## Recap of key points covered in the book

Throughout this comprehensive book, we journeyed through the multifaceted world of data science and big data, exploring concepts, techniques, tools, and ethical considerations underpinning the data-driven landscape. From understanding the fundamental definitions of big data to delving into advanced analytics and emerging technologies, we've navigated the intricate terrain of data analysis and its implications for diverse industries. As we conclude our exploration, let's recap the key points covered in this book, highlighting the pivotal insights illuminating our understanding of this dynamic field.

We began by delving into the very essence of big data— its volume, velocity, variety, and the inherent challenges it poses. Recognizing the distinct types of data— structured, semi-structured, and unstructured—we established a foundation for comprehending the complexities and opportunities presented by the massive amounts of information generated and collected in today's digital age.

Transitioning into the realm of data science, we unveiled its pivotal role in deciphering insights from big data. The data science lifecycle, exemplified by the CRISP-DM framework, provided a structured approach to extracting value from data, showcasing the iterative processes of data understanding, preparation, modeling, evaluation, and deployment.

Our journey took us through the intricacies of data preprocessing, illuminating the significance of data cleaning, transformation, and feature engineering techniques. These processes served as critical gateways to ensure data quality, enhance analysis accuracy, and prepare the dataset for subsequent stages of the analysis pipeline.

Exploring exploratory data analysis (EDA), we learned how visualization techniques bring data to life, unraveling distributions, patterns, and correlations. EDA emerged as a fundamental practice to unveil insights, fostering a deeper understanding of the data before embarking on advanced analytics.

Venturing into emerging technologies, we discovered the transformative potential of AI and machine learning in data analysis. These technologies empower data scientists to automate processes, enhance accuracy, and unlock new dimensions of insights across industries. We also explored various descriptive, diagnostic, predictive, and prescriptive analytics techniques that drive decision-making and innovation.

Ethical considerations loomed large as we examined big data usage's ethical and societal implications. The responsibility to safeguard privacy, mitigate bias, and ensure responsible innovation underscored the need for thoughtful practices that balance innovation with respect for individuals and society at large.

Opportunities abound in the dynamic landscape that awaits future data scientists, from interdisciplinary collaboration and responsible innovation to continuous learning and innovation. Yet, challenges such as information overload, data security, and privacy concerns demand vigilance and expertise to navigate the complexities of data-driven endeavors.

As we conclude this book, we've journeyed through the fundamental concepts, techniques, and considerations that define the realms of data science and big data. From grasping the significance of data preprocessing to understanding the transformative potential of AI and machine learning, we've explored the spectrum of insights that shape the landscape of data-driven decision- making. Armed with a comprehensive understanding of these elements, you're now poised to embark on your own data-driven endeavors, navigating the complexities, seizing opportunities, and ensuring that ethical considerations guide every step toward a future where data insights lead toward innovation, progress, and positive societal impact.

## Encouragement for readers to continue exploring data science and big data analysis

As we conclude this comprehensive exploration of data science and big data analysis, the journey is far from over. The world of data-driven insights is boundless, brimming with opportunities for innovation, growth, and transformative impact. As you stand at the crossroads of knowledge gained and the endless horizon of discovery ahead, let this encouragement serve as a guiding light, urging you to continue your exploration and immersion into the realms of data science and big data analysis.

Data science and big data analysis are ever-evolving disciplines; the only constant is change itself. The technologies, tools, and techniques that define this landscape are in a perpetual state of advancement, opening doors to uncharted territories of knowledge and understanding. Embrace the spirit of lifelong learning as you navigate these frontiers, staying abreast of emerging technologies, methodologies, and best practices. Pursuing knowledge is not a destination, but a journey that enriches your capabilities and enhances your contribution to the field.

Curiosity is the engine that propels innovation. Allow your curiosity to guide you as you explore datasets, ask probing questions, and seek insights that may be hidden beneath the surface. The most groundbreaking discoveries often emerge from unanticipated angles, where your curiosity leads you to explore uncharted avenues and unearth previously unnoticed patterns.

Data science and big data analysis come to life when applied to real-world scenarios. Engage with industries, organizations, and challenges that resonate with your passions. Whether it's healthcare, finance, environmental sustainability, or any other domain, your expertise can catalyze positive change and drive impactful solutions. Immerse yourself in the intricacies of these fields, collaborating with domain experts and data professionals to make a tangible difference.

Collaboration is the heartbeat of data science. Engage with fellow data enthusiasts, experts, and professionals who share your curiosity and drive. A collaborative community's collective wisdom and diverse perspectives can accelerate your learning, broaden your horizons, and spark innovative ideas. Effective communication—translating complex insights into relatable narratives—is equally paramount. Empower non-technical stakeholders with insights that inform decision-making and drive meaningful change.

As you embark on your journey, carry the torch of ethical and responsible practices. Uphold the principles of transparency, fairness, and accountability in every facet of your work. Recognize the societal implications of data usage and ensure that your contributions align with values that prioritize individual rights and the greater good.

In this realm of exploration, there is no one-size-fits-all approach. Each data scientist's journey is as unique as their fingerprint. Whether you're drawn to deep dives into data engineering, cutting-edge machine learning, or crafting impactful visualizations, forge a path that resonates with your strengths, interests, and aspirations. Your journey is yours to shape, and the possibilities are limited only by your imagination.

As you continue your expedition into the world of data science and big data analysis, remember that every challenge you encounter is an opportunity for growth, every insight you uncover is a stepping stone toward innovation, and every ethical consideration you uphold contributes to a better future. The discoveries you make, the solutions you create, and the positive impact you enable have the potential to shape industries, enrich lives, and make the world a better place. So, embrace the journey with open arms, for the adventure ahead is bound to be as exhilarating as it is rewarding. The path you tread today will lay the groundwork for a future where data-driven insights lead the way toward progress, innovation, and positive transformation.


## Final thoughts on the significance of mastering big data for effective analysis

As we reflect upon the journey through the vast landscape of big data analysis, the significance of mastering this field becomes increasingly clear. Big data isn't just a buzzword; it's a monumental shift in understanding, interpreting, and leveraging information. Our everyday data generation presents a wealth of potential that must be unlocked through effective analysis due to its sheer volume, velocity, and variety. In this final thoughts, we delve into the profound significance of mastering big data for effective analysis, exploring how it transforms industries, informs decisions, and shapes the future.

The mastery of big data analysis can revolutionize industries across the spectrum. Healthcare professionals can harness data to predict disease outbreaks, tailor treatments, and enhance patient care. In finance, data-driven insights refine investment strategies, mitigate risks, and optimize financial operations. The manufacturing sector employs predictive analytics to streamline production processes and minimize downtime. Big data fuels innovation, efficiency, and competitiveness from agriculture to entertainment.

Decisions can no longer afford to rely on gut instincts in a world driven by data. Mastering big data equips decision-makers with a comprehensive understanding of trends, patterns, and correlations, enabling them to make informed choices. Real-time data analysis empowers organizations to pivot swiftly in response to market shifts, customer preferences, and emerging opportunities. Whether it's adjusting marketing campaigns, optimizing supply chains, or responding to public health crises, data-driven decision-making is the cornerstone of effective leadership.

Mastering big data goes beyond the present—it extends into the realm of anticipation. Data scientists can assume future trajectories by analyzing historical data and current trends, allowing organizations to adapt strategies, products, and services proactively. Anticipating future needs can provide a competitive advantage in a constantly changing global environment, ranging from stock market patterns to consumer demand forecasting.

Big data analysis fuels innovation by providing insights that spark creative thinking. By identifying gaps in the market, unmet needs, and emerging trends, data-driven insights serve as catalysts for ideation. Organizations can harness this knowledge to develop novel products, services, and solutions that address pressing challenges and offer unique value propositions. Mastering big data transforms data into a canvas for innovation, where ideas flourish and boundaries are pushed.

The significance of mastering big data extends beyond commercial gains—it ripples through society, driving progress and positive change. From climate change mitigation to urban planning, big data analysis empowers governments and NGOs to make data-driven decisions that enhance quality of life. In healthcare, data insights guide public health policies, epidemics response, and resource allocation. The mastery of big data can foster a world where decisions are grounded in evidence, policies are shaped by insights, and societal challenges are met with data-driven solutions.

As we conclude this exploration of big data analysis, the overarching significance becomes abundantly clear. Mastering this field isn't a mere skill—it's a transformative capability that reshapes industries, drives innovation, and empowers decision-makers to steer the course of their endeavors with precision and vision. In an era where information is abundant and complexities are vast, the power of insights derived from mastering big data is unparalleled. The journey requires diligence, curiosity, and a commitment to ethical considerations, but the rewards are immeasurable. By embracing the significance of mastering big data for effective analysis, you're positioning yourself as a data professional, an architect of progress, an enabler of innovation, and a steward of informed decision-making that shapes a brighter future.

*Thank you for buying and reading/ listening to our book. If you found this book useful/ helpful please take a few minutes and leave a review on the platform where you purchased our book. Your feedback matters greatly to us.*